PRINCE:
A Practical Handbook

PRINCE:
A Practical Handbook

Ken Bradley

Butterworth-Heinemann
Linacre House, Jordan Hill, Oxford OX2 8DP
A division of Reed Educational and Professional Publishing Ltd

ℛ A member of the Reed Elsevier plc group

OXFORD   BOSTON   JOHANNESBURG
MELBOURNE   NEW DELHI   SINGAPORE

First published 1993
Reprinted 1993, 1994, 1995, 1996

British Library Cataloguing in Publication Data
A catalogue record for this book is available from the British Library

ISBN 0 7506 0587 1

Library of Congress Cataloguing in Publication Data
A catalogue record for this book is available from the Library of
Congress

Printed and bound in Great Britain by Clays Ltd, St Ives plc

Contents

Contents

About the Author

Ken Bradley has drawn his knowledge of the practical implementation and use of project management methodologies gleaned from over fifteen years in the field of project management, to create a readable and easily understandable interpretation of the PRINCE methodology.

He designed and delivered the initial training for Government departments in the GOVERNMENT PROMPT II methodology (the precursor to PRINCE), and has been involved in training and consultancy support for PRINCE since its introduction in 1989.

He is one of the four founding partners of Park Place Training, the leading provider of PRINCE training and consultancy support. His approach to using the PRINCE methodology is realistic and practical. It is this, more than anything else, which distinguishes the style of this book from others, and provides an essential companion for today's project manager and project team.

Acknowledgements

The writing of this book owes a lot to the encouragement, advice and help of Ken's other partners at Park Place Training, Poole. Ken also wishes to thank Colin Bentley for his comments on the draft of the book. Colin was one of the original directors of Simpact, the company which created PROMPT II from which PRINCE has evolved.

Introduction to Project Management

Definition of a Project

Before diving into a book about a project management methodology, we ought to define what we mean by a 'project'. There are many definitions around, but as a starting point, let us take the following:

'An event in which a group of resources undertake a series of activities in order to produce one or more end-products.'

This may be fine as far as it goes, but you could say that the day-to-day work done by an accounts clerk or production line meets these criteria. So we need a tighter definition.

Essential Characteristics of a Project

A project is unique. In some way at least, it is a one-off. Either the end-product has never been produced before, or not here, not by this team of people, not under these constraints ... and so on. It also has defined start and end dates. The end date is often imposed on the project, rather than being derived as a natural result of planning the activities. This makes it a constraint. Constraints are another attribute of projects. Other constraints might be money, equipment, locations or use of resources.

Another element which causes a project to differ from every-day work is that it is always the agent of change. Projects introduce change. Whether it is a new chemical plant or an extension to your house, a project results in a changed world.

The statement containing the end-products (or deliverables) required, the target date and constraints is often called a list of objectives. Apart from those which we have mentioned, there may be other objectives. An example would be the quality required.

Areas of Typical Failure

Many projects fail to:

- establish that there are good business reasons for undertaking the work
- keep the final client consulted and involved at every step
- identify the required end-products in sufficient detail
- define how satisfactory completion of each product will be measured
- identify and control all the necessary activities

- accurately estimate the effort required for an activity
- make allowance for work interruptions and non-project activities
- leave any allowance for poor estimating or things going wrong
- control the many changes to requirements which will occur

The Need for Project Management
In order to be judged as successful, a completed project must be:
- on schedule
- within budget
- complete with all the functions defined by the user
- of suitable quality

The chance of satisfying these requirements without control are remote. A project management method will provide much of the control needed, but the use of a standard development method which lists the activities to be done, their sequence and how they should be done also helps the planning and control of a project. For IT projects a set of development tasks and techniques such as SSADM might be chosen. SSADM stands for Structured Systems Analysis and Design Method and is the chosen technical method for government IT projects. The use of a method which defines what technical work has to be done merges neatly with PRINCE which looks after the planning and control aspects.

Avoiding Problems
If the work is to be done on schedule and within its budget it is essential that:
- The management levels above the project manager, including the client management, accept the fact that the project manager's plan should not be overridden without very good justification. Such justification does not include such phrases as 'I understand your plan shows that it can't be finished until September, but we need it by July, so get on with it.' How many project managers have met that attitude! But the trouble is, what do you do when confronted with that attitude? I have been told by many people that outright refusal to accept the impossible target simply means they will be replaced in the project by someone willing to say that it can be done, and a black mark placed against their name which will never be removed.
- The correct attitude entails checking that the plan was realistic, and if so, then re-examining the requirements. It is often possible to deliver the main requirements by the stated date, with lower priority needs following on from subsequent projects. An example might be the provision of day-to-day functions with specialist, annual and/or quarterly functions coming along later. This is a better approach than

steamrolling over the project manager's plan. As the saying goes, wishing doesn't make it so. Accept what can sensibly be done within the timeframe. In my experience on projects where a project manager's advice has been ignored and a reduced timeframe (or budget) imposed which is not backed up by a detailed (and credible) plan, an unsatisfactory product will result. This may be because corners have been cut, quality checks not carried out, work rushed and so on. If this is the result, then the managers who insisted on the abbreviated timeframe have only themselves to blame, not the project staff.

- All changes to requirements are identified, assessed for impact, and a joint understanding reached on what action to take. Agreement to incorporate the change implies agreement to increase the plan timescale and budget to cater for the change.
- Any change to the developer's ability to meet the specification is registered as soon as possible, discussed with the client, and a decision made.

No team member decides to exceed the requirements without obtaining the agreement of the project manager. One of my colleagues remembers taking over a project nearing its conclusion and discovering that for the previous two months two team members had been working away at changing some facilities from batch to on-line without the knowledge of the previous project manager!

Potential problems should be notified to the project manager at the earliest possible moment. The earlier the warning, the more reaction time there is. There is little worse than being told of a problem when it is too late to react to it – particularly if the problem was known by someone earlier.

Elements of Project Management
Project management consists of a number of activities:

planning
   the estimation of effort and duration
   scheduling resources to activities and dates
authorisation
   the review and approval of plans
   definition of how much of the project should be planned
monitoring
   recording actual time and costs
   the measurement of actuals against plan
   evaluating the quality of products being generated
   maintaining user involvement throughout the project
replanning and rescheduling
change control

These activities are expanded in the following sections.

Estimation

Systems development is an expensive and time-consuming business. It is reasonable that the person or company paying for the development should be given an idea of the investment they will have to make before sanctioning the project. But an estimate cannot be made with any great hope of its being correct until the work involved is known in considerable detail. The detail needed for an accurate forecast is unknown until the user requirements have been specified in detail, but the information is needed at the beginning of the project, before any large expenditure on it has taken place.

Many project managers are pressured into giving an estimate on the spot, as soon as they are handed the project. This is totally wrong. Subconsciously the project manager knows the user/manager wants to hear words like 'soon' and 'cheap'. Making an instant estimate when most of the requirements have not been identified in any detail, the normal human response is to see none of the difficulties, assume everything will go according to plan, and give a figure which ignores half of the work needed and all of the problems which will no doubt be encountered. But having been given such a figure, this is the one which the user and manager remember, the one to which they will continually refer, no matter what caveats you think you gave at the time about its being a rough idea.

I remember when I used to give programmers from a national company a project estimation job to do, they would come up with a ridiculously low figure. When questioned, they would admit that the time they had offered represented the time it would have taken them to write and test the two, three or four programs which they had identified as being required to solve the problem I gave them. They had made no allowance for all the other work in the project, such as specification, design, acceptance testing and so on. They had also based it on their doing the work, rather than ask any questions about the staff who would be allocated to the project.

The problem in estimation is, then, to produce time and cost estimates at the beginning of a project which will bear some resemblance to the final actual figures. At the same time, the user must be told of the margin of error involved in the estimate and the basis on which the estimate was made. It is therefore necessary to adopt a methodical approach to estimation.

There are a number of methods of estimating the size of effort needed for an IT project. If we ignore the wet finger in the air, we are left with:

- by experience
- by Function Point Analysis (Albrecht and Gaffney, Behrens)
- by algorithm
- by breaking the development process down into its constituent parts

and estimating each part separately

PRINCE will help with the latter, and the results of this over many projects could be translated into algorithms. As we shall see, as we study PRINCE planning steps, the process is concerned with breaking a project down into delivery of the required products.

Scheduling

The purpose of scheduling is to allocate activities to individual resources on specific dates. In order to do this, the activities must have been defined and put into a sequence.

In preparing a schedule, there are a number of factors to consider, such as:

- statutory holidays
- the possible learning curve of a resource
- project work which does not appear in the plan, such as telephone calls, ad hoc meetings
- sickness
- holidays
- repetitive work not appearing in the plan, such as filling in timesheets, replanning, writing out work assignments, appraising team members about their performance on recent work
- interruptions from non-project work
- smoothing out resource utilisation to avoid large peaks and troughs

Tolerance

No plan has ever been made where the actuals match the estimates precisely. Some things will go faster than expected, others more slowly. A resource will perform better than anticipated or worse. Unexpected problems will arise. (In one project on which I worked, an excavator dug up some telephone lines in Denmark, putting us out of touch with the German part of the project for some time.) It is also possible that you have forgotten an activity. All of these things conspire to deviate the actuals line away from the planned line. But at what point do you say 'this plan is out of control'?

Tolerance is the amount of deviation on either side of the planned line of schedule and cost which is permitted whilst still considering the plan to be under control. It is agreed between project manager and the management team for whom the work is being done. Any move outside the tolerance zone should ring alarm bells, cause a replan and ask for a new decision on whether to continue or not.

Effective Time and Management Time

Many plans fail because they have assumed two things:

- people are available 100% of their time to do project work
- the activities shown in the plan are the only project work which has to be done

No-one is 100% effective on a given project. There are interruptions from colleagues, visits to the coffee machine, sickness, non-work conversations and a hundred other items each of which takes a tiny sliver of a person's effective time. There are also many small project tasks which do not appear on a plan; the weekly team meeting, filling in a timesheet, an unexpected phone call or meeting with a user, a call to go and fix a problem with an operational system. All of these eat into the time available, time when team members cannot be doing the job which is shown in the plan for them. If we insist that they are 100% available to do only the activities which are in the plan, we have built an unrealistic plan which we do not have a chance of achieving.

There are two ways to tackle this. We can reduce a person's availability by a percentage which we feel might be eroded by all the reasons given above. For example, if we say that a person's genuine availability is 70%, then an activity requiring seven staff days would last ten days (duration = effort/availability). Alternatively we can add these ad hoc activities to our plan and allow a small percentage of total effort against them. An example here might be an activity called 'meetings' for which we allow 5% of each team member's time and 10% of the project manager's time. If this is done for the frequent time-taking, non-planned activities, it has the same effect of reducing a person's availability to do the planned activities. A software planning and control tool can really help this way of judging real effective time. This second method takes more time, because it is expected that time will be recorded against these administrative or 'hidden' activities. But this does have the advantage of providing statistics on how much time does go on the various categories, enabling you to improve your estimates for the next plan.

It must also be remembered that project management activities them-selves take time; creating plans, recording what actually happens, replanning, making sure everyone knows what they should be doing, checking on quality and the use of standards, ensuring that communications are maintained with all parties, and so on. It is a frequent mistake in plans that insufficient time is allowed for these activities. Many of the activities for the project manager are so small that they are not entered onto the plan. But they occur so frequently that they consume a large amount of time. Allowance must be made for these activities. There is a great danger in overscheduling the project manager with technical activities.

Software Planning Tools

Many software packages are available to help with planning, scheduling, recording actuals and reporting. The right one can make the creation of a plan much faster and relieve the project manager of a lot of drawing and re-drawing. The wrong one can consume an enormous amount of effort to learn or not contain the facilities required for the type of project in hand. You need to make a list of requirements before evaluating these packages. Cost is usually a small factor, especially if the package is to be used on many projects. Questions to ask include:

- *Ease of use.* How natural to your way of working are the moves through the software? A good package will include context-sensitive help and some kind of menu selection to guide you through all the necessary choices. Once proficient, there should be short-cuts to facilities via function keys. Can you create macros of frequently-used strings of commands?
- *Training.* What training is offered, and in what form? There are some pretty dreadful computer-based training packages being offered with some of the tools, very inflexible to the trainee's needs. In my experience a course with a teacher is far better. It is usually more cost-effective than believing you can teach yourself by picking up the software and starting to use it. I have seen a lot of such 'self-teachers' who only know about 10% of the package after months of working with it. They usually haven't found any of the short cuts or more powerful features.
- *Resource/activity.* Can you bring all a resource's activities together to record progress (very useful if you are extracting the details from a timesheet) or do you update individual activities?
- *Help in Plan Preparation.* How easy is it to fine tune or modify a plan? Are there graphics facilities to move things around, change their size and immediately see the effect of the change? What features does it contain to help you ask 'what if' questions?
- *Scheduling.* All the present tools will produce a plan within resource constraints. Some will only schedule forward, a few will schedule backward, a smaller number will offer to schedule without resource constraints and show any resource overcommitment. Will the software schedule an activity across differing levels of availability, including periods of non-availability? Some packages will include a defined overtime limit in scheduling to a fixed target date, and some will use a pre-defined alternative resource in trying to achieve a target date. Remember that the more sophistocated the package, the higher the cost, the longer the learning curve.
- *Reporting.* Can you only use a standard set of reports or create your own? Can the package provide the graphic reports you would like?

- *Multi-project.* Do you have a need to combine projects, hive part of a plan off into a separate plan, link information from one project plan to another?
- *Resources.* Does the package only handle human resources, or can it accomodate materials, costs and any others you use?
- *Product and Supplier Reliability.* For how long has the product been available? Is this the first version? Is it from a reputable supplier? How many users are there? Is there a User Group? Can you talk to any current users?
- *Capacity.* How many activities does it support? Is there a limit on the number of resources it can handle? How many rates can be held for any resource? What time periods can it handle?
- *Facilities.* Does it draw network diagrams? Does it produce bar charts? Does it show resource availability, utilisation, unused availability? Can you view different aspects of the plan at the same time? How good are the graphic displays of each aspect? If you make a change, can you see the effect immediately? How easy is it to change any aspect of the plan? Does it contain functions which will schedule the plan for you? Does it allow you to set baselines? How clearly does it show actuals against plan?

Assessment and Authorisation

When a plan has been scheduled and costed it is not automatic that it should go ahead. The plan must be reviewed against the objectives and any constraints. The project management method should define who will assess the plan, the procedure to be followed in order to assess it and the data against which it should be assessed.

Should the plan be outside the constraints, such as time or money, the review must consider its options. Examples of these are:

- stopping the project
- accepting an increase in time or cost
- reducing the scope of the plan
- lowering the level to be achieved (performance, quality)

With regard to authorisation, the project management method should not only define who must approve a plan, but what plans must be produced for approval. For example, there will be a recommendation to break a project down into a number of plans, what type of plans are required, what constraints should determine the size and scope of a plan.

Monitoring

The purpose of monitoring is to:

- check that work is proceeding according to plan
- check that work is being done to the standards required

- spot any deviations at the earliest possible moment and take corrective action
- reschedule all or part of the work as necessary

In order to achieve these things, activities should be broken down into small units of work, no more than a handful of days. Human nature has a tendency to believe that it can catch up on any slippage, make a breakthrough tomorrow, and will often only confess to being behind schedule when the day comes when the work should be finished. Breaking work down into small pieces means the early reporting of any failure to meet schedule.

Estimates of time to complete should be by date or days of effort. Experience has shown that when staff are asked to estimate a percentage complete, this tends to be over-optimistic.

Actual effort should be logged on time sheets by team members at frequent intervals, say half daily. I have seen many project team members fill a time sheet in for the whole week immediately prior to its being handed in. Usually accurate figures have not been kept, so it is guesswork as to how much time was spent on activities, particularly those done early in the week. This doesn't help identify the accuracy of the original estimate or improve future estimation.

Change Control

Failure to identify and control changes to either the specification of the project's end products or the ability of the development team to meet that specification is usually catastrophic. There must be a procedure to record all such requests, assess their impact, and make a decision on the action to take.

Start by assuming that only the person or group paying for the development can authorise the incorporation of any changes or make any other decision regarding proposed changes. Other decisions might be to cancel the request or defer the change to a later enhancement project. The second point is that changes should not be incorporated into the current plan, to be done without increase in time, cost or effort. Any decision to include a change should go hand in hand with agreement to increase the plan to accomodate the extra work.

For each proposed change there needs to be:

- a description of the change and reasons for it
- an assessment of the impact that making the change would have on other products and on the plan
- the cost and schedule implications
- an evaluation of the need for and priority of the change
- a formal, signed decision from the funders of the project

Rescheduling

As actuals are recorded, there needs to be a regular measurement of progress against what was planned. Where deviations are identified, there will be a need to replan and reschedule to adapt to the changing situation. The planning network is a great help at such times. It identifies the Critical Path; the sequence of activities through the plan which have no spare time; and how much spare time other activities have. Rescheduling covers possible switching of resources, allocating extra resources, changing the sequence of events, deciding to have some resources work overtime. The need for rescheduling in order to meet targets is very difficult, if not impossible, to identify if no plan exists against which to measure actual progress.

The Approach Taken by This Book

So how should a project be constructed so that it encourages:
- the setting of clearly defined objectives
- client involvement, particularly at management level
- accurate assessment of the project's economics
- accurate estimates of resource needs
- the avoidance of large expenditure until the viability and practicality of the project have been proved
- sufficiently careful monitoring that any changes to expectations are quickly identified and cause a controlled, documented and communicated response?

You can probably begin to list the essential ingredients of a good project management method from these questions. This book examines such a method, PRINCE.

This book takes the PRINCE elements and tries to look at them in a natural order for the project manager. It avoids the duplication of the current five-volume set from the CCTA, but covers all the components fully – and fills in a few gaps left in the current volumes.

The chapters are presented in a sequence ready to take a project manager through a project. Where possible, particularly in the planning steps, a simple example is used to help show how the techniques work.

PRINCE Overview

This chapter looks at the PRINCE definition of a project, the background and pedigree of PRINCE, its current use and the official documentation. It then discusses the components of PRINCE, products, activities, plans, controls and organisation, and how they combine to cover the needs of project management.

Project Organisation
This chapter discusses the needs and purpose of having a formal organisation with which to undertake a project. The PRINCE standard organisation structure is presented, with definitions of the roles. From experience a number of ways of implementing the structure are suggested. This includes ideas on the establishment of a Project Support Office as well as variations on the use of the Project Manager/Stage Manager roles.

PRINCE Plans
This chapter includes a section on the wisdom of breaking most projects into stages for the purposes of detailed planning. Before getting into plans at project and stage level this chapter explains the PRINCE steps in producing a set of plans at either level. This includes the Product Breakdown Structure and Product Flow Diagram steps before the Activity Network. A simple non-IT example is used to take the reader through the processes, including 'transformation'. The chapter also relates to elements which should appear in the plan description, such as plan risk analysis, assumptions, external dependencies, quality plan, contingency level and so on. Where the item will be fully covered elsewhere in the book, this is indicated. Otherwise a full explanation is given here.

Project Initiation
This looks at the major management control point of getting a project off to a business-like start. There are cross-references to the components already mentioned, such as organisation and plans. A full description is given of other topics, including Business Case, Project Brief and Acceptance Criteria.

The description of the development of the Project Plan continues the simple example from the previous chapter and uses it to explain the detail required. The level required for the Quality Plan is defined, plus the need to include the Configuration Management Plan.

Having got the Project Technical Plan, the reader is introduced to the PRINCE flexible concept of stage selection. Reasons for having stages are discussed. The simple example is brought back to be a basis for the discussion.

The steps to develop a Stage Plan in detail from the Project Plan are also described in this chapter.

Monitoring and Reporting
This covers the PRINCE controls of Checkpoint meetings and reports, Highlight Reports. It also ties the PRINCE requirements to plan updating and suggests a package of documents to make the two controls complete.

Controlling the Products

This chapter describes Configuration Management, the concepts behind it, the job of the Configuration Librarian in terms of controlling the products and their descriptions. Product Descriptions are explained, as is how these relate to the quality aspects in the next chapter.

Controlling Quality

Quality Reviews are dealt with in detail, the process, roles, agenda. Informal reviews are described, as are the links to the various plans.

Controlling Change

Technical Exceptions are covered, together with roles and suggested procedures. The link with plan deviations is defined, ready for that chapter. Exception Memos are also introduced.

Stage Assessments

The intention of End Stage Assessments is tied back to the idea of project stages. The objectives, participants, their roles are all clearly explained.

Controlling Deviations from Plan

Mid Stage Assessments, Exception Plans and the triggers for them are defined.

Project Closure

The various Acceptance Letters are here, plus making sure that the status of all Requests For Change and Off-Specifications has been clarified. The chapter goes on to look at the Project Evaluation Review, the assessment of what lessons should be learned from the project and a measurement of the project against its Acceptance Criteria. The holding of the project closure meeting is described. It ends by looking at the Post-Implementation Review.

Appendix A Product Breakdown Structures

This offers a hierarchical structure of the products of a typical computer system.

Appendix B Product Descriptions

All the products shown in Appendix A (and a few more lower level products) have sample Product Descriptions provided.

Appendix C Organisation Roles

There is a job description for each defined role in PRINCE.

Appendix D Activity Lists

Lists are provided for the important management activities, such as Project Initiation.

Appendix E Sample Form Layouts

The PRINCE guides from the CCTA do not offer form layouts. Instead their Product Descriptions are provided. These descriptions have been taken and turned into sample layouts which the reader could use either as they stand or modified to specific department or company standards.

Glossary of Terms

A glossary of all PRINCE terms.

1 | PRINCE Overview

PRINCE is a further development of PROMPT II, the proprietary project management methodology which was adopted by the CCTA in 1979 as the standard for government IT departments. PROMT II was developed by a company called Simpact Systems, later taken over by Learmonth and Burchett Management Systems. The CCTA has added a number of enhancements and changes to the original methodology and has put the resulting PRINCE methodology in the public domain.

PRINCE is a methodology for management of any type of project, not just for computer system development. It is, however, designed to be compatible with the system development methodologies used in government IT projects, and accomodates their use for the technical aspects of development. Because it has begun life as a method related to IT projects, the Technical Product Descriptions in the CCTA PRINCE manuals and Appendix B of this book reflect the products required in the development of a computer system.

The CCTA have published through NCC Blackwell a five-volume guide to PRINCE. The five volumes are

> Introduction to PRINCE
> PRINCE Management Guide
> PRINCE Technical Guide
> PRINCE Quality Guide
> PRINCE Configuration Management Guide

These are comprehensive, but expensive. The five volumes are intended for the different levels of readership. There is thus a certain amount of duplication of information between the five volumes. The guides do not attempt to teach project management principles, simply setting out the PRINCE approach to the various elements. This book tries to condense into one all the various aspects of PRINCE and relate each point to basic project management needs. In this way it is hoped that it will appeal to those needing to understand project management as well as those wanting to know about PRINCE.

Definition of a Project

In the CCTA volume, 'Introduction to PRINCE', a project is defined as having:

- a defined and unique set of products
- a corresponding set of activities to construct the products
- appropriate resources to undertake the activities
- a finite life-span
- an organisational structure with defined responsibilities

Project Aims
There are four major aims for any project:
- to deliver the required end-product(s)
- to meet the specified quality
- to stay within budget
- to deliver on schedule

PRINCE Project Management Components
From this description it is easy to trace the PRINCE philosophy that project management must be built around:
- the products required by the client (or user)
- the activities needed to produce those products
- a method of planning which starts from the required products and incorporates the derived activities
- a series of controls also based on those products which cover quality, schedule and cost
- an organisational structure which defines the essential roles, responsibilities, levels of decision-making and lines of communication, all interlinked with the other components described above

The Products Component
At the core of PRINCE is the definition of the products to be produced by the project. Not just the final products, such as a software system, user manual and training material, but all the products which have to be created on the way to that final system. For example, if the final product is a new washing machine, before that can be achieved a prototype has to be built, which needs a design, which will be based on a specification and so on. From the list of all the products required on the way to the end-product(s) we can derive the sequence in which they have to be produced and the activities required to generate those products. Also as part of the description of each product the quality criteria are defined, which will be an important part of our control.

When asked to identify the products of a project, the normal reaction is to list the technical products. But PRINCE divides consideration of products into three:
- management
- technical

- quality

This is done so that the planner will deliberately consider the management and quality products (and activities) required. Without this many plans are produced containing simply the technical activities and an apparent assumption that management and quality work doesn't take any time or consume any resources.

Management Products

Management products are any contracts or agreements, all the plans, approvals of them and reports against them.

Quality Products

Quality products cover statements of quality policy, quality procedures, all the definitions of quality criteria, product reviews and all the documents leading from the reviews. They provide, among other things an audit trail of the quality goals, intentions, quality checking done and the results of that checking.

Technical Products

The technical products required by the end user should be defined at the start of the project in a Project Brief. Additional technical products may be required by a technical strategy which is appropriate to a particular part of the project. Appendix A shows the content and structure of products of a typical computer system development project, and can be used as a basis for such projects.

The Activities Component

The required activities are derived from the products and their sequence. If the steps of the previous component have been carried out correctly, this will yield management, technical and quality activities.

Management activities are concerned with planning, monitoring and reporting the work of the project. Any activities needed to create products such as contracts or agreements with outside parties are also management products.

The quality activities cover two things. Any testing work can be regarded as quality work. In PRINCE there are also specific Quality Reviews, meetings to inspect a product or partial product and ensure that it conforms to specification and quality criteria. By making the planner think about quality activities, it is less likely that the time and resources for these will be omitted from the plan.

The technical activities describe the work needed to produce the technical products of the project.

PRINCE isn't trying to be pedantic with its insistence on separating management, technical and quality products and activities. The aim is just to ensure that thought has been given to management and quality work. Without this thought, far too many plans are created which ignore them and the effort they will require.

The Organisation Component

Some of the major complaints about projects in the past were that the user didn't feel fully involved, wasn't kept in the picture, and didn't have any real control of the expenditure of the budget. PRINCE attacks these problems by providing an organisational structure and standard set of job descriptions. These identify the user role in all decisions from major expenditure, requirements specification, and design approval to requests for change. Apart from this they also show lines of authority, communication and responsibility for all key activities in a project.

The Plans Component

Planning and replanning are important project management activities. PRINCE provides a structure for preparing and maintaining plans at appropriate levels throughout the life of a project. Plans are prepared for the Project as a whole, for each stage within the project and for detailed work within each stage. There is also an Exception Planning process to handle deviations from the original plan. The PRINCE structure addresses the need for technical planning, resource planning and quality planning.

Technical Planning

Technical Plans are concerned with the products to be delivered and with the activities necessary to ensure that the products emerge on time and to the required quality standards.

- The Project Technical Plan outlines the major activities of the project. It is used with the Project Resource Plan to provide the Project Board with an idea of the total cost and schedule of the project before commitment of major expenditure. Later it is used as a comparison with actual progress on the project. It also defines project policy related to Quality Control and Configuration Management.
- A Stage Technical Plan shows in much greater detail than at project level the products, activities and quality controls of each stage of the project. The Stage Technical Plan is produced and approved at the end of the previous stage (the plan for the first stage is prepared as one of the inputs to getting approval to go ahead with the project).
- Detailed Technical Plans can be used where required to give a detailed breakdown of particular major activities within a stage, e.g. system testing.
- Individual Work Plans are extracted from the Stage and Detailed

Technical Plans to allocate specific activities to members of the Stage Team.

Resource Planning

Resource Plans are summaries of the budget and resources needs of the project. They are derived from the corresponding Technical Plan.

- The Project Resource Plan identifies the type, amount and cost of the resources required by the project for each stage.
- A Stage Resource Plan defines in more detail the resources required by a particular stage. It defines the budget and resource needs both cumulatively and for each relevant time unit, normally weekly. It is also used to report actual expenditure and resource usage against plan.
- Detailed Resource Plans will be produced when required to define the needs of a particular major activity.

Quality Planning

It is inadequate to believe that a good quality product will be produced automatically. For a start, what do we mean by good quality? The meaning of quality taken by PRINCE is 'fitness for purpose'. There must be documented agreement between user and developer on what both understand by quality. Technical terms such as 'mean time between failure' and 'mean time to repair' might be used. In PRINCE quality criteria have to be defined and agreed for all project products. Quality Review procedures must be established and the intended review activities must be defined and resourced.

The effort needed for quality activities must be integrated into the Technical and Resource Plans at each level and described in the plan text.

The Project Level plan lays down the overall quality strategy for the entire project. It defines the standards and procedures to be followed and the quality criteria for the major products. It also documents the developer's understanding of the priority of quality in the user's mind compared to cost and time.

At stage level the quality plan contains the quality criteria, test methods and review guidelines of each product to be produced during the stage. Specific quality reviews are planned and ideally the resources to be used for them named. As a minimum the chairman of each formal quality review should be identified.

If there is a detailed plan this will require a quality plan similar to one for the stage plan.

Exception Planning

The Project Board and project manager agree a tolerance level for each stage plan. This defines the limits of timescale and cost variation from the plan within which the project can operate without further reference to the Project Board.

An Exception Plan is required in situations where costs or timescales have already exceeded, or are likely to exceed, the tolerance level set by the Project Board. The Exception Plan describes the cause of the deviation from plan, its consequences and recommends corrective action to the Project Board. Once approved, the Exception Plan replaces the remainder of the current stage plan.

The Control Component

Regular and formal monitoring of actual progress against plan is essential to ensure the timeliness, cost control and quality of the system under development. PRINCE provides management and technical controls to monitor progress, supported by a reporting procedure which enables replanning or other corrective action to be taken.

Management Controls

PRINCE provides a structure of management controls to be applied throughout the project. These controls cover all aspects of project activity and, at the highest level, allow senior management to select moments in the project when they can assess project status prior to committing further expenditure. Controls are applied via meetings of project management and project staff, with each meeting producing a set of pre-defined documents. There are five key management controls:

Project Initiation

to provide a controlled start to the project, ensuring that the terms of reference, objectives, plans and job definitions are clearly defined, understood, agreed and published. It also has the function to verify that a reasonable business case exists for the project and that any risks have been studied. The major management control points are established and the frequency of reports.

End Stage Assessment (ESA)

This is a mandatory management control and occurs at the end of each stage. It consists of a formal presentation to the Project Board of the stage results, the current project status and a request for approval of the Resource and Technical Plans for the next stage. Project Board approval must be obtained before the project can proceed in other than a limited way (see MSA) to the next stage.

Mid Stage Assessment (MSA)

This is similar in many ways to the End Stage Assessment. It has the same attendees; the Project Board, Project and Stage Manager plus Project Assurance Team. It can be held for a number of reasons:

- if the stage is a long one (say, more than eight weeks) the Project Board may begin to feel a little remote and out of touch. The Mid Stage Assessment gives face-to-face meeting to review the status;
- if the stage has or is about to deviate beyond its tolerance levels, the Project Manager has no authority to continue. There must be a Mid Stage Assessment at which an Exception Plan is presented in order to obtain approval to continue the stage;
- a Mid Stage Assessment can also be used to authorise limited work to begin on the next stage before the current stage is complete.

Checkpoint Meeting

This is a technical control point held regularly, usually weekly, with the stage team. Checkpoint meetings can be conducted by the Team Leader, Stage Manager or on his behalf by the Project Assurance Team. The main aims are to gather information to measure actual achievement against the Stage Technical Plan and review any current or potential problems.

Highlight Report

This is a written report from the Project Manager to the Project Board. the frequency is laid down by the Project Board. The PRINCE manuals suggest that the frequency is decided at the time of Project Initiation, which will normally be satisfactory. A typical period would be every two weeks or month. But the Project Board can change the frequency from stage to stage, depending on the length of a stage or the risk involved or criticality of that stage. The report consists of a summary of the Checkpoint Reports received during the period plus brief details of the current budget status.

Project Closure

This is a final review of the project by the Project Board when the system has been accepted by the user. They receive a report from the Project Manager on the achievement of the original objectives, the status of the installed system and a review of any lessons learned for the benefit of future projects. Based on the results of this meeting the Executive reports back to the IT Executive Committee.

Product Controls
Quality and Technical controls are applied to specific products. The aim is to examine products and correct any errors as early as possible in the development process.

Quality Review
A Quality Review is an inspection method carried out by a group using formal roles, procedures and documentation. These must have been defined in the project quality plan. They form an important part of the audit trail of quality work. At each Quality Review, appropriate technical and user staff are designated to examine a product to ensure that it is complete and correct. The product is reviewed against defined quality criteria to assure its technical integrity and its compliance with user requirements.

Technical Exceptions
A Technical Exception is a question or description of an unplanned situation relating to one or more products. Examples are any changes which the user requests or any inability to produce a product to its specification. In order to keep any divergence from specification under control, it must be recorded and action agreed.

Configuration Management
A Configuration Management Method (CMM) helps control the development of products by providing a formal mechanism for labelling them, tracking their development status, and recording any relationships between them. It also provides secure storage for completed products, controls access to them and finally releases the complete system. If the system is installed in several locations, the CMM stores details of each installation and version details.

2 | Project Organisation

Introduction
In the Introduction to this book we talked of the need for any project management methodology to keep the client consulted and involved at every step. This is one element which we see addressed in the Organisation component. User involvement is defined at two levels; at a management level, monitoring and approving expenditure, and at the every-day working level, answering questions on user needs, how things work, and checking that the development stays in line with user needs.

Possible Project Organisation Environment
PRINCE concerns itself in detail with the organisation for a single project. The CCTA PRINCE Management Guide does, however, spend a little time describing what the environment might look like beyond the single project. This looks at the links between a development project and the setting of IT strategy.

Figure 2.1 shows the PRINCE view of the business environment and surrounding management structures in which computer projects would be undertaken. If you are looking to PRINCE for use with non-computer projects, the philosophy is the same. Just change the references from Information Technology (IT) to the appropriate group for you.

At the top of the company or department there could be a group responsible for setting the strategy, looking ahead five to ten years and deciding what their business world will look like and what role they see for their company. They will plan a strategy to meet that view.

Below them PRINCE sees the need for a group to plan the Information Technology structure of systems which will be needed to support that future view. It calls this group the Information Systems (or Technology) Steering Committee (ISSC or ITSC), responsible for supporting the overall objectives of the business strategy group in terms of the information systems environment required. Figure 2.2 shows some of their work. The ISSC will require a hardware policy - one central, large computing facility or distributed processing? What role for micros? What teleprocessing needs? What supplier policy should they have? Similar questions regarding software policy and strategy, staffing and so on. In order to make decisions in these areas they will trigger off many studies, projects in

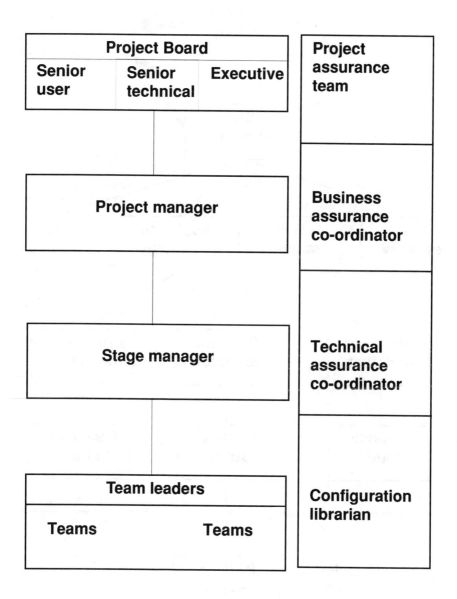

Figure 2.1 PRINCE Organisation Roles

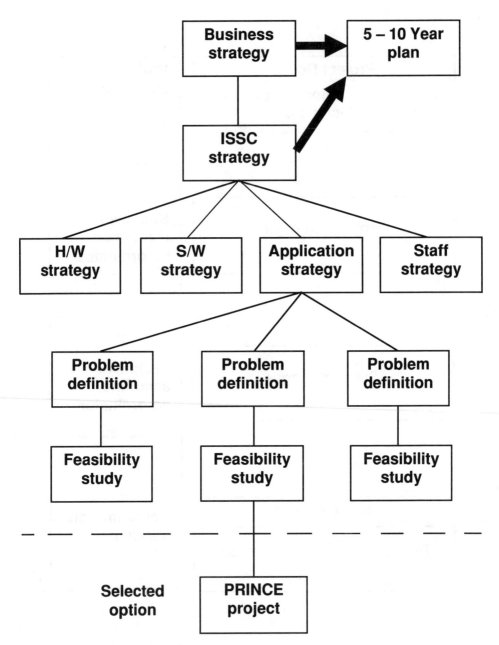

Figure 2.2 The work of the ISSC

themselves. In computer project terms these studies will consist of Problem Definition and Feasibility Study. Based on the results of these studies, the ISSC will draw up a list of required projects and priorities.

Apart from identifying requirements, the ISSC also has responsibility for the implementation, monitoring, review and tuning of its strategy. This all may result in too heavy a workload for the senior line managers who sit on the ISSC, and PRINCE proposes a sub-group, a planning secretariat (ISPS) to do a lot of the detailed work, reporting back to the Steering Committee.

The implementation of the ISSC's requirements is handed down to an Information Technology Executive Committee (ITEC), who have the job of balancing available resources against fulfilment of the ISSC strategy. In most companies this means that at any time there will probably be several projects in progress.

It would be normal for the head of computer services to be a member of the ISSC and head up the ITEC.

Again the ITEC, consisting of busy line managers, will not have the time to concentrate on every project. Thus they will appoint a Project Board (PB), responsible to them, for each system under development. A Project Brief is passed to the Project Board, giving terms of reference, any constraints, a guidance on tolerance levels and an idea of the project's place in the overall strategy.

Prince Project Organisation

We have now reached the point where PRINCE begins to define the organisation within a project. Figure 2.3 illustrates a project organisation. It now offers much more precise descriptions of the groups, teams and individuals.

PRINCE defines the required organisation of a project in terms of roles, rather than individuals. The same individual may play more than one role, or play different roles at different stages of the project. A role may be played by different people at different times of the project or shared, according to the project needs at that time. Formal role descriptions are given in Appendix C.

The Project Board

A Project Board is appointed to take overall control of a PRINCE project. It consists of three management roles, each representing major project interests. It is important that the roles are taken by managers, because they are required to make decisions and, more importantly, make commitments to the project. They sign off requirements and commit resources and budget, so the managerial level must be commensurate with the size of commitment required.

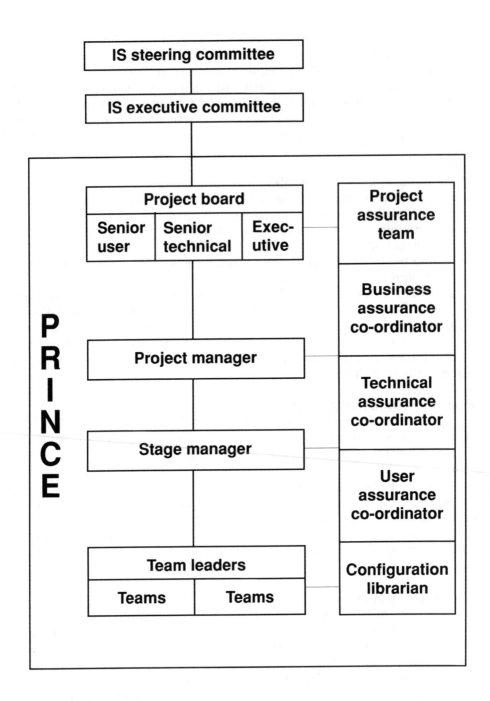

Figure 2.3 PRINCE Organisation

Executive

appointed by the IT Executive Committee to provide overall project guidance and assessment on behalf of the IT Executive Committee, formally bringing the Project Brief to the project and reporting back on the project outcome.

Senior User

representing users of the system or the major products from the project. If the system is to be used by more than one user area, the role can be shared. Care should be exercised not to take this to extremes. A dozen Senior Users would tend to make arrival at decisions a protracted affair. If a large number of user areas are involved, it would be sensible for them to identify, say, three representatives at the most to represent them as Senior Users.

Senior Technical

representing areas which have responsibility for technical implementation. Usually this requires a manager from the area which is to supply the development staff.

The Project Manager

The Project Manager role is the one to assume responsibility for day-to-day management of the project throughout all its stages.

The Stage Manager

In a large or complex project, the Project Manager may have Stage Managers assigned the technical responsibility to deliver the products of one or more particular stages.

Depending on the resources required and/or skills available, the Project Board may choose to appoint:

- one Project Manager, supported by a Stage Manager for each stage
- one Project Manager who also assumes the role of Stage Manager throughout
- a succession of Stage Managers, each assuming the role of Project Manager for the duration of the stage

One international oil company had a policy of using Stage Managers. For stages developing user requirements, testing the system for acceptance and installation they would appoint user managers to the role. For the design and development stages the Stage Manager came from the area which provided the development expertise.

Stage Teams

The Stage Manager is supported by one or more Stage Teams to carry out the activities and produce the technical products of the stage. The final level of authority in the organisation structure is that of Team Leader.

The Project Assurance Team

The Project Assurance Team (PAT) provide support functions in planning and control, standards, quality control, user liaison and product control. It consists of:

Business Assurance Co-ordinator
to provide expertise in the planning and control methods, maintain budgetary information and administer the quality control procedures.
Technical Assurance Co-ordinator
to provide guidance on technical standards and procedures, maintain technical assurance controls and monitor technical integrity.
User Assurance Co-ordinator
to represent the users' interests at every stage of the project and maintain user assurance controls.
Configuration Librarian
to control storage of and access to all the finished products of the project. This role keeps track of differing versions of the products as the system develops and is responsible for packaging the system for release for installation.

The Stage Teams will often change from one stage to the next, according to the skills and numbers required. The Project Assurance Team roles help provide consistency to the project by being involved from beginning to end. Having said this, it is possible to re-allocate the role of the Technical Assurance Co-ordinator to relate to the standards and technical advice needed for a particular stage.

Outside the PRINCE organisation for a project there are two other areas for consideration.

Project Support Office

A central Project Support Office within a company or department may provide staff for the Project Assurance Team, particularly the Business Assurance Co-ordinator and Configuration Librarian. In a working environment with a limited number of techniques and technical standards, sometimes the Technical Assurance Co-ordinator role can be supplied from a central group.

PRINCE Co-ordinator

To make the most effective use of PRINCE, each site should appoint a PRINCE Co-ordinator with sufficient authority and experience to act as trainer and internal consultant in the methodology. This role is often made part of the Project Support Office, if this office is to be used.

3 | PRINCE Plans

The Need for Plans

Some people still need convincing of the need to plan project work in detail. You can see them rolling their eyes and thinking to themselves, 'I could have had the job half done by the time I've finished planning it.' But even before the simplest of projects, say, a shopping expedition, it pays to sit down and plan it. What are you going for? What shops must be visited? In what order? Where is it best to park? You want to avoid buying the heavy items in the first shop and carrying them a long way back to the car. How much money will you need? How will you pay? Have you remembered the shopping trolley? I remember taking a one-day trip to France with my wife one winter. The local ferry company was offering tickets at one pound each. Off the boat we dashed straight to the supermarket, loaded a trolley with wine, beer, French cheese and other delicacies, and headed for the checkout. Outside the supermarket we realised that trolleys could not be taken out of the car park and we were half a mile from the boat. There were some very sore fingers and shoulders by the time we got there. How much better it would have been had I treated it like a project and planned it before rushing into it.

Here are a few reasons why you need to plan a project:

- to prove whether a target is attainable or not
- in order to say what it will cost
- in order to say how long it will take
- in order to identify potential problems in the implementation steps (Exactly what is involved? What could go wrong with this step? What products and tools will be involved?)
- to help answer the question 'is this a good investment of scarce resources?'
- as a basis for delegating some of the work to other resources than yourself
- to act as a communication document to others on the intended steps through the project, when these are expected to occur and how they relate to one another.

These are some of the reasons why you should plan before beginning a project. But once you have started the project, if it wasn't planned you can't properly control it. How can you answer the joint questions, 'where am I?' and 'where should I be?' without a plan? The plan becomes your measure of where you should be. Updating that plan with actuals shows you the impact of any problems. Replanning helps you to react to any problems.

But how much time should you spend in planning? What should be the balance between planning time and actually getting the job done? Life is dynamic and ever-changing. All projects are subject to change. Not only would it be an incredibly long and arduous task to plan down to a handful of days all the individual tasks to be done by a team on a project due to last a year or more, you can bet that there will be many changes during that time which will amend all of those tasks, certainly the tasks more than a short period ahead of us. So why waste the time?

The answer is to have a flexible approach to planning which is dependent on parameters such as the duration and risk of the project. The whole project should be planned before beginning the project, but not necessarily in detail. The next part of the project to be done should be planned in detail, because without detailed planning, you can't have detailed control.

Recently I visited a marine engineering company who were having problems with their projects. These were coming in consistently late, over budget, and increasingly quality corners were being cut. I was shown a project plan by the (only) project manager. A project lasting fifteen months had been divided into about twelve major steps. The time scale was measured in months and a symbol was used to indicate in which months that work would be done. There were no figures of effort required, and the minimum duration for a step was shown as a month, with the average being two months. This was the only plan. There was no breakdown elsewhere of the work involved in any of these steps, no allocation to individuals. When I asked why there was no more detail, the project manager told me 'I only have five minutes a week to plan' and he might have anywhere between three and six projects running at the same time!

I asked him if he was finding out about delays to a step far too late to do anything about it, and whether (after the event) he found out that the staff had cut out one or two quality checks in order to try to recoup some of the lost time. He said yes and wondered how I had guessed. Often the quality had to be rectified by sending parts to wherever the boat was in the world, and occasionally sending an engineer out to repair the fault. When I asked if the company would take on a person to help him plan in more detail and capture actuals on a regular basis, the reply was 'the company wouldn't stand for the extra cost.' I wonder what was the true cost of continually missing deadlines, overrunning budgets and having occasional failures in quality?

We are now going to have a look at how PRINCE tackles the planning of a project, how it combines the high-level planning of a total project with the low-level planning of the next part to be done.

Levels Of Plan

Figure 3.1 shows the hierarchical structure of PRINCE plans. Each plan has a specific purpose, to establish control at a certain project level. All the plans except the Individual Work Plan comprise a technical plan (what are we going to do and how long will it take?) and a resource plan (what resources are needed and how much will it cost?).

- the *Project Plan* covers the entire project and provides a fixed reference point against which overall progress can be measured at the end of each stage
- when it has been decided (by looking at the Project Plan) into how many stages the project should be broken, a *Stage Plan* describes that portion in much more detail and is the basis for controlling that part of the project on a day-to-day basis
- if required, a *Detailed Plan* may be prepared to give a further break-down of an activity within a stage. It is not mandatory.

These three levels control the normal running of a project. If a Stage Plan becomes out of control, i.e. begins to move outside the tolerance margins set by the Project Board, an *Exception Plan* must be presented for approval by the Project Board, which runs from that moment to the end of the stage and replaces the Stage Plan. Any Detailed Plans and Individual Work Plans within that timeframe *may* have to be replaced.

The *Individual Work Plan* is simply an extract from the technical part of either a Stage or Exception Plan.

Project Plan

The Project Plan is created by the Project Manager during project initiation. It is a high-level sizing of the project, showing the major products to be created, their sequence and the number of resources which will be needed. It is not the objective to control the project on a day-to-day basis against this plan. The objectives of making a Project Plan are:

- to give a guide on whether the overall targets can be achieved
- to input to the business case an idea of how much the project will cost
- to help the Project Manager and Project Board decide into how many stages the project should be broken for planning and control purposes
- to provide a basis for planning each part of the project in more detail
- to provide a measure of progress at the end of each stage

Stage Plan

The plan for the first stage is prepared during Project Initiation by the Project Manager, assisted by the Project Assurance Team and, if the role

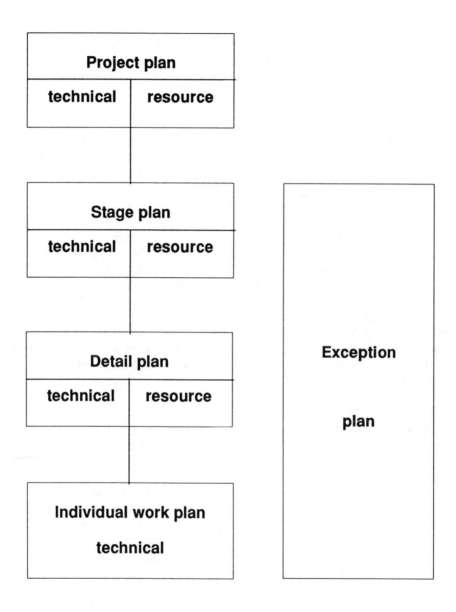

Figure 3.1 PRINCE plan structure

is used, the next Stage Manager. For the remaining stages, the Stage Plans are produced at the end of the previous stage. At the end of each stage the actual performance against the stage plan is reviewed by the Project Board as well as the plan for the next stage. Both are assessed against the project plan and any differences reconciled.

Detailed Plan

As an option, the activities to produce a complex or large product can be left as one long activity in the appropriate Stage Plan and expanded in their own Detailed Plan. As an example, the work to collect, clean and convert data might form a Detailed Plan within the Development Stage Plan of a computer applications project.

Individual Work Plan

As stated earlier, this is not a further level of detail, but an extract from either a Stage Plan or a Detailed Plan of the work to be assigned to one resource. Sensibly the extract covers only a short period, one product or a small number of activities to last two to three weeks. This is regularly refreshed as the stage moves forward. It gives the Project or Stage Manager the maximum flexibility in resource allocation, deciding on or changing resource allocation as events unfurl. Together with a graph of the work, the resource would receive details of the standard expected and method of quality confirmation.

Planning Steps

PRINCE provides a series of steps to produce a plan. The steps are the same for a plan at any of the levels mentioned earlier, the Project Plan, Stage Plan or Detailed Plan. Only the level of detail changes. The steps are shown in Figure 3.2. Not all the steps are mandatory. Only the Technical Plan (bar chart), Resource Plan and Summary Graph are essential. The others produce working documents which gradually build towards the essential documents, but they do represent an excellent way to create a plan.

In order to explain the planning steps we shall take a simple example. *Please note* – the example project is a very simple one, chosen so that the reader can concentrate on understanding the planning steps. At the end of the chapter, the same steps are shown for a typical IT project. We shall construct each step of a PRINCE plan for a small company which has decided to create a Christmas card containing a photograph and greeting from all the staff and send one to all its clients. They are going to do as much of the work themselves as is possible.

Project Level Plans

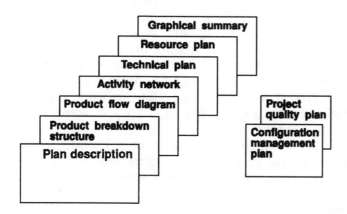

Stage Level Plans

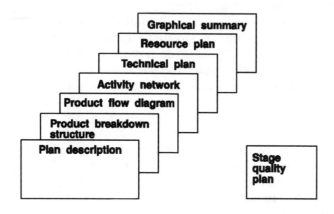

Figure 3.2 Planning Steps

Identify the Products

Most other planning methods ask you to begin a plan by thinking of the activities, and listing these in a hierarchical structure called a Work Breakdown Structure (WBS). PRINCE believes that the activities depend on what products are required to be produced by the project, and that the correct start point for a plan is to list the products. This is called a *Product Breakdown Structure*. Another important departure from other methods is the PRINCE emphasis that, apart from the Technical products of a project, there are always Management and Quality products. Listing these will remind us that they too take effort to produce and need to be planned as much as the production of Technical Products. In order to construct a Product Breakdown Structure, start with a box at the top of the structure showing what the final deliverable of the planned work will be, e.g. a system, a new yacht, a department relocated to a new building. At the next level down, list all its components.

Figure 3.3 gives an example of the start of a Product Breakdown Structure for the technical products of a typical software development project, showing the components of the final system. Depending on the level of detail required by the plan, each component may be broken down at subsequent levels.

It is rare in a project that work begins immediately on the final products. Interim products are needed on which the final products are based. For example, before the finished product there might be a model. Before the model there will be a design, and before that a specification. These are also products. So from the final products we work back through time, adding to the Product Breakdown Structure these interim products until we arrive at the products with which the plan starts.

With our example the final product will be 'Mailed Personal Christmas Cards'. We shall resist the temptation to say just 'Christmas cards' because the project won't be finished until the cards have been dispatched. Our title reminds us of some extra work after the cards are ready.

Thinking of the Technical Products, our final product consists of:

- fully prepared Christmas cards
- envelopes
- stamps

We can now add to this list by working back in time and asking ourselves of each product, 'What product(s) do we need in order to build this?' For example, the envelopes won't be much good unless they have a name and address on them, the card needs designing. Our list of Technical Products might end up looking like Figure 3.4.

The structure is an evolving one. Over the next steps, extra products will suggest themselves and be added to the structure.

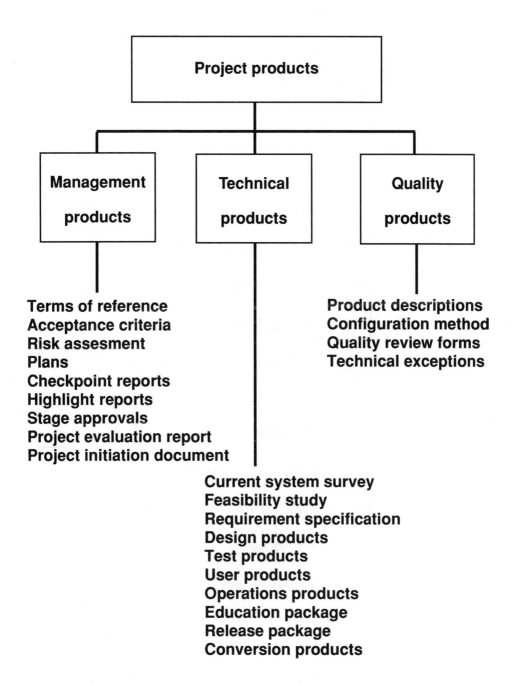

Figure 3.3 Product breakdown structure

Figure 3.4 Christmas card project list of technical products

Management and Quality Products

Having thought of the technical products, management and quality products should be listed. Management products include any contracts, all plans, control documents, progress reports, meeting minutes and approvals. As we shall see later in the book, an important management control at the beginning of every project is Project Initiation, where we make sure that there is good justification for the project and everyone knows their responsibilities. Quality products include all the quality checking documents and Product Descriptions. For our example the Management and Quality Products might look like those in Figure 3.5. PRINCE offers a general list of these products which can be used unchanged for most projects.

Management products	Quality products
Terms of reference Plans Plan approvals Reports Project initiation document	Product description Quality review documents Quality plans Technical exception documents

Figure 3.5 Management and quality products Christmas card project

Create Product Descriptions

For each identified product, at all levels of the Product Breakdown Structure, a description must be produced. The purposes of this are to provide a guide:
- against which the finished product can be measured
- to the author of the product on what is required
- to the planner in how much effort will be required to create the product

These descriptions are a vital checklist to be used at a quality review of the related products. The description should contain:
- the purpose of the product
- the products from which it is derived
- the composition of the product
- any standards for format and presentation
- the quality criteria to be applied to the product
- the quality verification method to be used

If we were to write a Product Description for the staff Christmas photograph in our example, it would look like:

Title: Staff Christmas Photograph

Purpose:
- to be the original from which copies can be taken for the company Christmas card
- to remind clients of the company name and services offered
- to help create a feeling of a more personal relationship between clients and members of staff
- to link the company and staff with the sentiments of well-being, friendliness and family in the eyes of clients.

Content:
- all staff
- company logo (either building, company van or overalls)
- Yuletide trappings

Derivation:
- staff list
- professional quality camera and film
- a dozen poses
- professional film development

Quality Criteria:
- sharp, clear photo of everyone and company logo
- prominent position of company logo
- everyone in clean, smart attire representative of their work
- everyone looking happy and waving at camera
- gives a general Yuletide feeling

Quality Verification Method:
Trial photos of proposed logo, Yuletide trappings and lighting to be used to be checked out before assembling staff. Final choice   Managing Director to select from one dozen poses.

Technical Strategy

No further planning should be done before an appropriate technical strategy has been worked out. The objectives of the technical strategy at the project level are to:
- deliver what is required
- make acceptable and efficient use of time and resources
- be consistent with project constraints
- be amenable to adequate control and management
- minimise risk of failure

The strategy should identify any standard methods to be used. For example, a software development might identify SSADM as its standard method. Will a package be bought in and used unaltered, or will it be developed from scratch by in-house staff? The strategy chosen will often affect the list of products to be produced, the sequence in which they are produced and certainly the way in which they are produced.

At a stage level any methods specific to that stage should be described in the technical strategy. Going back to our Christmas card project, the Technical Strategy might be to use one of the staff who is a keen amateur photographer and artist to keep costs down, but to use external resources for the printing and photographic development.

Quality Strategy

As part of completing the list of quality products to be produced in the plan, it is necessary to consider what quality strategy will be needed.

The quality strategy is there to:

- ensure that products are complete and correct
- detect errors at the point where the cost of correcting them is minimised

At the project level there needs to be a statement of what quality means to both user and developer. The PRINCE Technical Guide quotes BS 4778 as:

- 'the totality of features and characteristics of a product or service which bear on its ability to satisfy a stated or implied need.'

Quality needs to be related in importance to the other constraints of the project. Time, money and resource availability all affect quality. Other constraints and standards affecting quality should be described, including:

- documentation standards
- external constraints, e.g. quality assurance groups

The strategy should define any inspection and test methods to be used. The types of test to be carried out should be stated, and the major points in the project at which these will occur.

The definition of technical activities required within a plan is incomplete without the addition of quality activities and the resources to carry them out.

The major quality activities in the Christmas card project would be inspection of the design, the photos, the greeting and the finished card.

Draw a Product Flow Diagram

A Product Flow Diagram is then drawn, showing the sequence in which the technical products in the Product Breakdown Structure must be produced. Time flows in one direction only. The diagram begins with what is available at the start of the project and ends with the required final products (deliverables). In PRINCE any products which are expected to be already available or coming from outside sources are shown in an ellipse. All products to be created by the project are shown in boxes. The derivation of a product is shown by drawing an arrow to it from each of the products from which it is derived.

The objective is to further develop the technical strategy in terms of how the products are to be gradually developed, one from another. The sequence will be affected by the technical strategy which was documented earlier.

In tracing the product flow in this way, extra interim products may be identified which are required to build and support the final products. Products which exist outside the project and are needed in the building of the new products will also be discovered. For example, a Feasibility Study for it may have already been done as part of the overall strategy work, or a description of the current system or product may already exist.

After putting all the technical products into the Product Flow Diagram, the management and quality products are examined to see if they should be brought into the flow. Products such as plans, contracts and quality reviews should be added to the diagram. The previous comment about discovering extra products also applies to those needed to ensure the quality and management of the project, such as test, conversion and implementation strategies.

All extra products identified should be added to the Product Breakdown Structure.

Figure 3.6 is a Product Flow Diagram for the Christmas card project.

Identify the Activities

The CCTA manuals at this point talk about identifying the Transformations. This simply means taking the Product Flow Diagram and writing on it in the appropriate sequential place the activities which will turn one product (or set of products) into the next product (or set of products). For each target, ask the questions, what activities are needed to:
- change
- create
- ensure the quality

Figure 3.7 shows the activities to create the products of our Christmas card project.

Produce an Activity Network

The annotated Product Flow Diagram forms a very good basis for the development of an Activity Network. In fact, there are project managers who go direct from the previous step to the production of the Technical Plan without making an Activity Network. But a network is a useful aid to

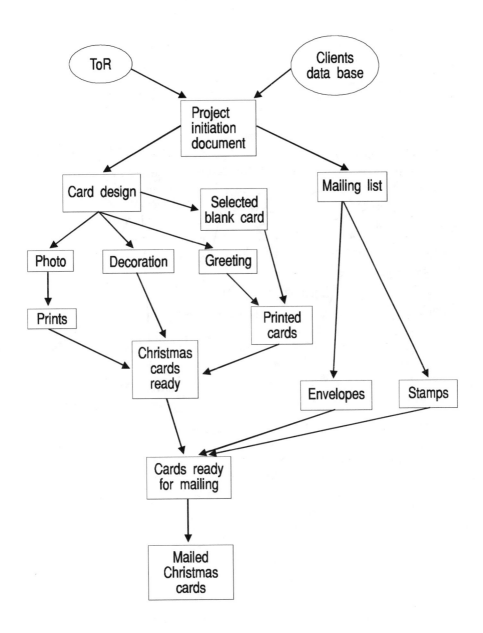

Figure 3.6 Product flow diagram

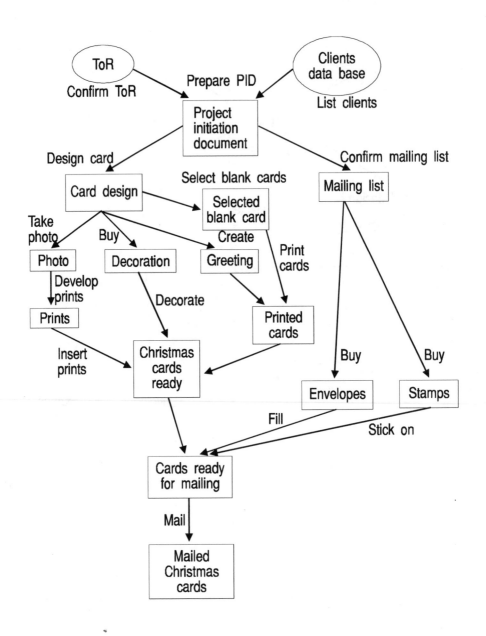

Figure 3.7 Product flow diagram & activities

the planner, because this identifies the Critical Path and activity Floats which help when scheduling and resource smoothing. It also offers a more formal basis for estimating the duration of the activities.

Figure 3.8 is an extracted list of the activities for the Christmas card project, showing the dependencies for each activity and our estimate of the duration of each. The time unit used is a quarter day.

Activity		Duration (0.25 day)	Dependencies
10	List clients	4	–
20	Confirm ToR	1	–
30	Prepare PID	3	10,20
40	Confirm mail list	1	30
50	Design card	4	30
60	Select blank card	1	50
70	Design greeting	4	50
80	Buy design materials	2	50
90	Take photo	1	50
100	Buy stamps	1	40
110	Buy envelopes	1	40,60
120	Print cards	8	60,70
130	Develop cards	8	90
140	Decorate cards	12	80,120
150	Insert prints	2	130,140
160	Prepare for mailing	2	100,110,150
170	Mail	1	160

Figure 3.8 List of activities – Christmas card project

Figure 3.9 shows a network of these activities. This book does not set out to teach the theory of network planning, but it is worth taking a moment to make sure the reader understands the network. Each activity is placed within a box. The box shows other information about the activities duration, start and finish dates as illustrated below.

Earliest Start Time	Duration	Earliest Finish Time
Activity Identifier and description		
Latest Start Time	Float	Latest Finish Time

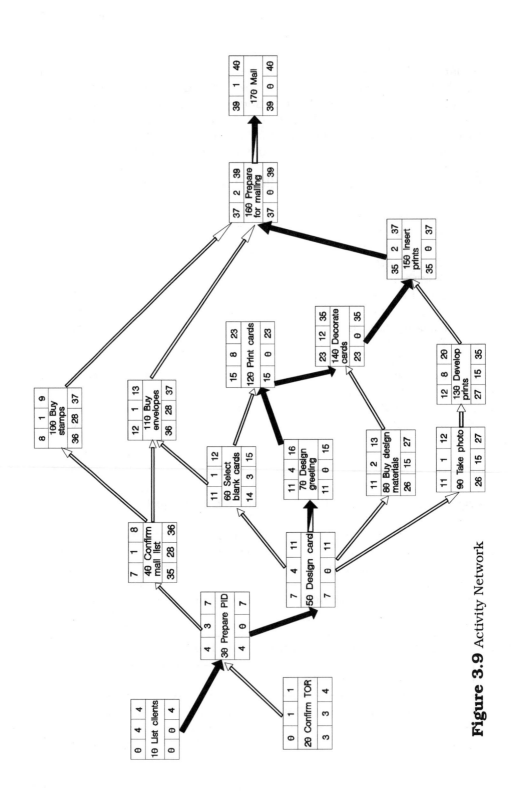

Figure 3.9 Activity Network

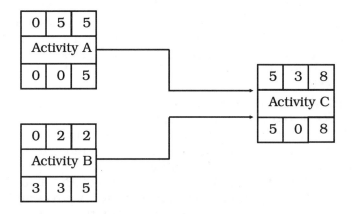

The Duration of each activity is added to its Earliest Start Time. The Earliest Start Time for the two activities right at the beginning of the network, numbers 10 and 20, is defined as zero. The Earliest Finish Time for one activity becomes the Earliest Start Time for the next activity and so on. Where an activity is dependent on more than one previous activity, its Earliest Start Time is the latest Finish Time of its predecessors. As an example of this, activity 110, 'Buy envelopes' depends on two activities, 40 ('Confirm mailing list') and 60 ('Select blank cards'). Activity 60 will occur the latest of the two predecessors and will finish at the earliest after 12 time units. Activity 110 can be done any time after that. But the activity which follows that, number 160, 'Prepare for mailing', cannot start until activity 150 is also finished. This will not happen until after 37 time units. Since activity 110 only requires one time unit to do it, it can be done any time within the next 24 time units without delaying activity 160.

Working through the network from left to right gives the total duration of the plan. Working backwards through the plan, subtracting each duration, tells you which activities have any spare time (known as 'float'). For example, let us say activities A and B can be done simultaneously and both have to be done before C. A needs five days, B two and C three. The whole job will last eight days and B has a 'float' of three days. B could start up to three days late or take three days longer without delaying the start of activity C.

Creating the PRINCE Technical Plan

At this point the PRINCE manuals become rather vague. The Management Guide says that the next steps are to identify constraints, management and technical control points and resources. It suggests that resources can be allocated to activities and timescales defined, all using the planning network. As the network is not drawn against a timescale, these tasks are very difficult to carry out using this document as a basis. It is much easier to transfer the network to a bar chart.

In practice the bar chart can be considered the Technical Plan. It must be accompanied by the Plan Description in order to be complete. The Plan Description is covered later in this chapter.

An Activity Network is fine as far as it goes. It shows the sequence of events, which activities can be run in parallel, the estimated effort for each activity, the total duration of the plan, critical path, floats, earliest and latest start and finish times. What more do we need? But if done properly the network does not take into account how many resources are available. It shows the minimum elapsed time provided there are no resource constraints. Networks also find it difficult to answer such questions as:-

- where will we be in January?
- what will Mary be working on in June?
- how heavily loaded is Harry?
- we started a month ago. Where are we now?
- are there any peaks or troughs in my resource utilisation?

In order to answer such questions we need a plan which is laid out against a timeframe. Figure 3.10 shows our simple network transferred to a bar chart.

Before moving on it is worth checking the management and quality columns in the Product Breakdown Structure for any on-going activities which did not appear in the Product Flow Diagram but which will require time and resources. Examples are weekly checkpoint meetings, preparing Highlight Reports, the End Stage Assessment and the Configuration Librarian's work. These must be added to the bar chart.

Resource Allocation

Before beginning resource allocation, resource availability should be considered. Many plans make the mistake of assuming that a full-time team member will do five days' project work each week. A human being is less than one hundred percent efficient and many interruptions and events will occur which are not in the plan; telephone calls, ad-hoc meetings, work discussions, chats at the coffee machine and so on.

Each project needs to decide what effective percentage of time each member will spend on project work. there are two major aspects to this:

1.   how much of that person's time is allocated to that project?
2.   for how much of that allocated time will the person be doing work which appears in the plan?

I know of several projects in the Northern Ireland DHSS where the project

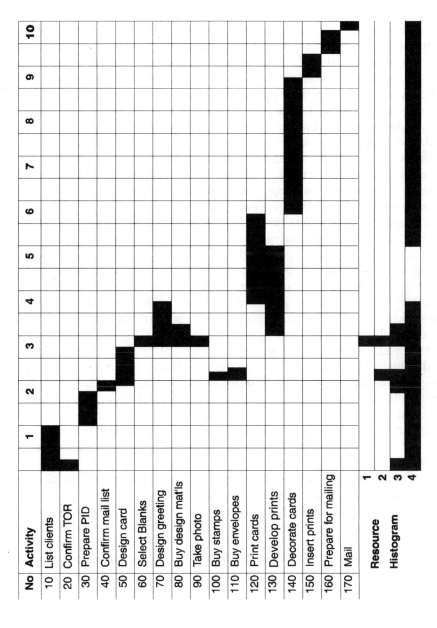

Figure 3.10 Technical plan – Christmas card project

staff were doctors, nurses, ambulance crew, caterers; people who could only be spared for one or two days a week to do project work. Now reduce that figure by a percentage to allow for unplanned project work, remembering where they were last time they worked on the project, little meetings or phone calls which are not in the plan! On another occasion the IT department of a national utility company told me that they kept careful track over a considerable period of how much time they were spending on activities which were in their plan. They were horrified to find out that they were only 40% 'efficient'. And yet those plans were assuming them to be 100% available! In other words, 60% of their time was going on project activities which did not appear in the plan, telephone calls, conversations, meetings, and so on. No wonder they had problems keeping anywhere near their schedule. They were not inefficient. They had simply not realised that there are many small activities which go on every day which do not appear in plans, but which erode the time.

The best way to find out how much effective time people can give to a project is to record and analyse how time is spent and draw conclusions. If project staff have spent 10% of their time in unplanned meetings in the past, is there a reason to believe this will change for your project? Many sites have tasks such as 'meetings' running throughout a plan with an estimated % of each member's time allocated. Another example is 'planning and monitoring' for the project manager. Time is booked, and over a period the planner gets to know where time is being spent and how much.

Even if you are using a software planning tool, the best way to approach the allocation of resources to activities is to produce a bar chart first. The rule for resource allocation is *in order of ascending float*. This means start with the first activity on the critical path (which has a zero float) and allocate resource(s) to it. If there are still resources available and activities which can be done in parallel, allocate resources to activities, following the above rule, until either the resources are all occupied or no more activities can be started yet. Then wait until a resource is free and the network dictates that another activity can begin. If there are sufficient resources at each point, then the Technical Plan may show that you can achieve in reality what the network showed in theory. But if there are insufficient resources to carry out all possible parallel activities, the Technical Plan will take longer than the network showed.

There are times when a resource with a specific skill must be used for particular activities. This has priority over the above normal allocation steps. The need to wait for the availability of a specific resource may adversely affect the overall time required for the plan.

Resource Smoothing
After the first pass at resource allocation it is useful to view the resource

usage for each time period (column). In the interests of efficiency the aim is to have the smallest number of resources used on a continuous basis consistent with the opportunities for parallel activities shown in the network. Figure 3.10 shows a first pass at a Technical Plan. The histogram of resource utilisation is very ragged; high resource usage one minute, half the team doing nothing the next.

Using the float information from the network, activities not on the critical path can often be delayed within their float, decreasing the maximum resource number needed and taking up some of the wait time without extending the target completion.

After smoothing there may still be some wait times, resource usage may still be excessive, or the end date for the project may now be too late for the sponsor. If so, the terms of reference and constraints must be examined to see what the priorities are. Where meeting an earlier target date is most important, the logic of the Activity Network can be reviewed for more possible overlaps of activities, enabling more effective use of resources and bringing forward the forecast end date. Such action will increase the risks to the project and will need to be properly assessed and documented by the Project/Stage Manager before presentation to the Project Board.

Going back to our Christmas card project, Figure 3.10 was a Technical Plan which assumed we had sufficient resources to do the activities as soon as the network said they could be done. In fact, for a short period there were four resources in use. If we employed resource smoothing here, we could produce Figure 3.11. By delaying non-critical activities within their float, we don't use more than two resources, and yet the project is accomplished in exactly the same overall time.

Calculating Resources and Costs

The resources used now need translating into costs. This means that any resources other than the human ones, such as machine time, consumables, new equipment, must be identified. Any administration costs not shown in the Technical Plan must also be listed and quantified.

Figure 3.12 gives an example of a Resource Plan. The requirements for each different type of resource for each time unit are totalled and translated into costs. The costs are accumulated to give a running total across the plan. If the plan covers several years, it is normal to identify the anticipated inflation rate and increase future years' costs by this amount.

The total resource type needs and costs should be checked against the constraints provided by the Project Board. Any excess may require re-planning or negotiation with the Project Board.

Resource Plan Graphical Summary

PRINCE asks for a graphical summary of each Resource Plan. This is a

No	Activity	1	2	3	4	5	6	7	8	9	10
10	List clients	■									
20	Confirm TOR	■									
30	Prepare PID		■								
40	Confirm mail list		■								
50	Design card			■							
60	Select Blanks			■							
70	Design greeting				■						
80	Buy design mat'ls				■						
90	Take photo				■						
100	Buy stamps				■						
110	Buy envelopes					■					
120	Print cards		external								
130	Develop prints		external								
140	Decorate cards									■	
150	Insert prints									■	
160	Prepare for mailing										■
170	Mail										■

Figure 3.11 Technical plan (two resources)

Effort	Stage 1	Stage 2	Stage 3	Stage 4
Ken Harper	1.75	1.25	3	0
Assistant	0.25	0.5	1.25	1.35
Total effort	2.00	1.75	4.35	1.25

Costs	£	£	£	£
Ken Harper	350	250	600	0
Assistant	25	50	125	125
Computer	10			
Sub-Total	385	300	725	125
Printing		25		
Development		25		
Materials		20		
Stamps/env		100		
Total	385	300	915	125
Cumulative	385	685	1600	1725

Figure 3.12 Project resource plan

simple graph with Time and Cost axes. At project level the time axis is divided into the project stages. At stage level it uses a relevant period of time such as a month, according to the total duration of the stage.

An example of a Project Resource Plan Graphical Summary is shown in the next chapter.

Plan Description
The foregoing plans provide details in graphic and tabular form of the planned work and expenditure. In order to fully understand the plan the Project Board will also require a piece of text. This document is the Plan Description and contains:
- the purpose, approach and general philosophy of the plan
- any assumptions made in the production of the plans (e.g. specific resources, their availability, their skill levels, facilities available, the ability to meet target dates of any external resource or contractor)
- any plan pre-requisites (what must be in place before the plan can begin e.g. programmers recruited, training carried out, equipment installed, work by external resources completed)
- any risks embedded in the plan. At the level of a Project Plan this will be a separate document, the Business Risk Assessment. This is

covered in detail in the chapter dealing with the creation of the Project Plan. At a stage level part of the Plan Description will be an assessment of any risks embedded in the plan. This is an important subject and is therefore covered in detail in the chapter on planning a stage.

The following is an example of the Plan Description as it might read for our Christmas card project.

Project: Client's Christmas card

Plan Description:

Purpose:

The purpose of this plan is to show the work and cost needed to produce and mail a Christmas card to all company clients.

Background:

Although sales are healthy, repeat business has shown a slight decline in recent months, and management are concerned to keep the company name and its services in the mind of all client buyers. Rather than yet another sales flier, management feel that the approach of Christmas allows the opportunity to put our name in front of the people who matter in a manner where we are seen not to be continually dinning them for more business, but appreciative of our association and wanting to send them good wishes. A greetings card which personalises our staff should help produce the image desired by management of a company where clients deal with real people who want to help them.

Approach:

Young Ken Harper from the design office is a keen amateur photographer. In keeping with the image sought by management, this plan seeks to use his skills to design and hand-craft a greetings card which will be clearly the personal creation of this company's employees, rather than one bought from an outside source. In order to produce a high quality product, external professional resources will be used to develop copies of the chosen photograph and print the greeting on the card.

Assumptions:

1. Ken Harper will be made available for the effort shown in the plan.
2. A further resource capable of neat, clean work will be found to support Ken.
3. Ken will be able to use his own photographic equipment without cost to the plan.

4. All staff can be spared at short notice for a photographic session lasting 30 minutes.
5. An extract can be easily made from the company computer data base of all our clients.
6. There will be a period of dry weather during the working day on or within a day of the planned time.

Pre-requisites:

1. All blue collar workers will be provided with new overalls for the photograph.

Plan Risks:

1. There is no suitable weather for an outside photograph. As a contingency an internal shot could be taken in the garage, using the company van to display the logo. But the garage walls are an unacceptable backdrop to the photo. A professional developer could substitute a different background, but this would be at extra cost.
2. The Managing Director might not like any of the poses. Any ideas held by the MD on what is wanted or not wanted should be expressed on paper as part of the Terms of Reference.
3. There could be a delay at the printers. A slot could be booked in advance to avoid this.
4. There could be a delay at the developers. Again a time could be booked with them.
5. As the plan relies on the availability of Ken Harper, any illness or late holiday on his part could jeopardise the plan. The plan should be begun as soon as possible to give maximum leeway in case of illness, and Ken should be asked not to take holidays until the plan is complete.
6. As the activities are small and of a type well known to the project staff, a tolerance of only 10% will be allowed.
7. The project manager will report on a weekly basis to the Project Board. The report will consist of a Highlight Report and a tabular report on schedule and cost against plan.

Typical IT Project – Sample Planning Steps

The following pages (Figures 3.13 – 3.20) show the products of the various PRINCE planning steps. The example is taken from a case study used on one of our training courses. The Gantt Chart (Figure 3.16) and planning network (Figure 3.17) were produced by the PMW (Project Manager Workbench) planning and control software from Hoskyns Group, a product which we often use to help with our projects. The Product Breakdown Structures in Appendix A can also be used as a guide to the start point for an IT product.

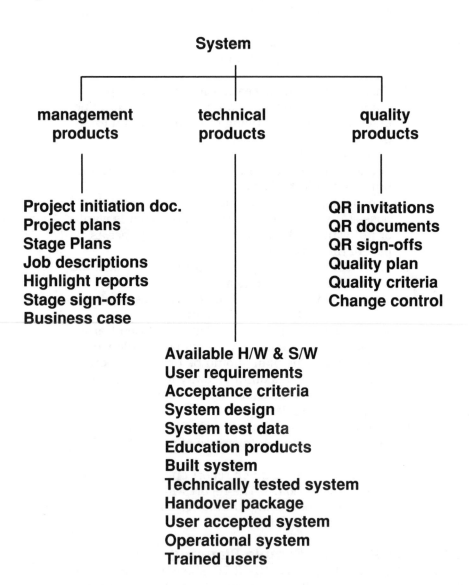

Figure 3.13 PRINCE case study – product breakdown structure

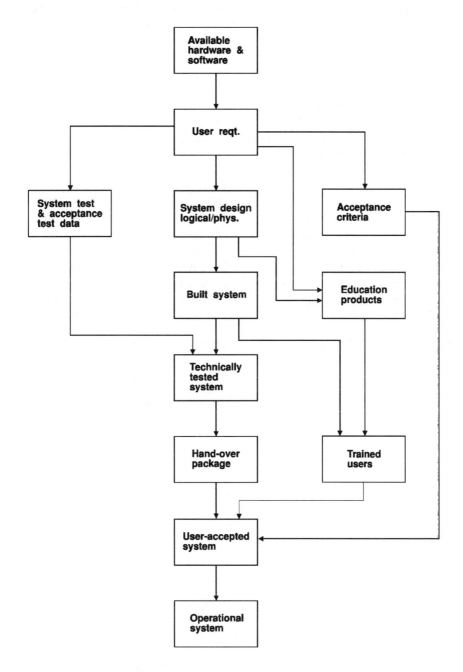

Figure 3.14 PRINCE case study – product flow diagram

Description of activity		Duration	Dependencies
05	Plan & Prepare the PID	8 days	–
10	Define current system	12 days	05
20	Produce user requirement	15 days	10
30	Produce education strategy	5 days	20
40	Produce acceptance strategy	10 days	20
50	Produce system test data	7 days	20
60	Produce acceptance test data	10 days	20
70	Produce logical design	8 days	20
80	Produce physical design	15 days	70
90	Build system	18 days	80; 50
100	Carry out system tests	5 days	90
110	Produce training package	12 days	30; 80
120	Produce handover package	4 days	100
130	Train system users	15 days	110
140	Carry out acceptance tests	10 days	120; 90; 130; 60; 40
150	Tune the system	10 days	140
160	Deliver system & sign-off	5 days	150

Figure 3.15 PRINCE case study – activity network

PMAC case study	Day	Resrc
05 Plan & Prepare PID	17	I U O
10 Define Current System	27	I U O
20 Produce User Reqt	30	I U O
30 Produce Education Stra	6	U O
40 Produce Acceptance Cri	11	U O
50 Produce Systest Data	15	I U O
60 Produce Accept Test Da	9	U I
70 Produce Logical Design	7	I U
80 Produce Physical Design	10	I U
90 Build System	25	I U O
100 Carry Out System Test	14	I O
110 Produce Training Pack	14	I U O
120 Produce Handover Pack	4	I O
130 Train System Users	23	I U O
140 Carry Out Accept. Test	10	I U O
150 Tune The System	12	I U O
160 Deliver System & Sign	4	I U O

Legend

||||| Activity   CIIIII Activity on critical path

Figure 3.16a Cantt chart – PRINCE case study (page 1)

PMAC case study

	Day	Resrc	June 1990			July 1990					August 1990				September 1990				October 1990				Nov
			14 21 28	4 11 18 25	2 9 16 23 30	6 13 20 27	3 10 17 24 1	8 15 22 29	5

Resource summary

Utilization

IT Resource	10.0	I	5.0 3.5 2.1 2.0 2.0 1.6 1.5 8.2 7.0 3.4 2.7 2.0 6.7 6.3 6.3 6.1 5.2 4.4 3.1 0.5 1.0 3.0 2.6 0.8	
User Resource	10.0	U	3.2 3.5 8.5 8.2 7.2 6.6 6.5 9.3 10.0 9.1 3.5 0.4 2.6 2.0 3.2 3.8 3.2 1.2 0.7 3.5 3.1 1.5 1.4 0.8	
Other	7.5	O	2.5 1.7 1.0 0.7 1.7 1.6 1.5 2.6 1.5 0.2 4.5 4.3 4.0 4.6 4.9 2.7 1.2 1.0 1.1 1.5 1.6 1.6	

Total days			10.7 8.7 11.6 10.9 10.9 9.8 9.5 20.1 18.5 12.7 6.2 2.4 13.8 12.6 13.5 14.5 13.3 8.3 5.0 5.0 5.2 6.0 5.6 3.2	

Figure 3.16b Gantt chart – PRINCE case study (page 2)

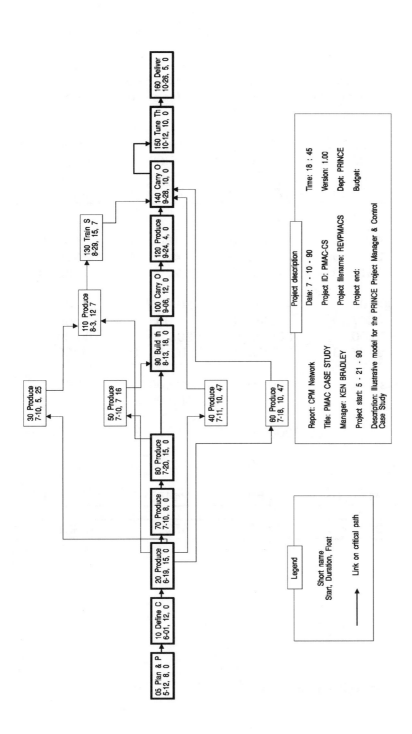

Figure 3.17 CPM network – PRINCE case study (page 1)

Day rate User 100   IT 120   Other 110
Management overhead   10%

	–Stage 1– plan	actual	–Stage 2– plan	actual	–Stage 3– plan	actual	–Stage 4– plan	actual
Staff effort								
Man days								
User	44.00		33.00		18.00		11.00	
IT	18.00		37.00		35.00		11.00	
Other	11.00		5.00		25.00		8.00	
Total	73.00	0	75.00	0	78.00	0	30.00	0
Staff costs								
User	4400	0	3300	0	1800	0	1100	0
IT	2160	0	4440	0	4200	0	1320	0
Other	1210	0	550	0	2750	0	880	0
QR costs	300.00		400.00		300.00		300.00	
Manage'nt	807	0	869	0	905	0	360	0
Proj Board	600.00		300.00		300.00		300.00	
Staff total	9477	0	9859	0	10255	0	4260	
Computer costs			500.00		2200.00		300.00	
Hardware					12000.00			
Software								
Environ't			1000.00					
Other								
Computer total	0	0	1500	0	14200	0	300	0
Stage total	9477	0	11359	0	24455	0	4560	0
Cum. plan	9477		20836		45291		49851	

Figure 3.18 Project resource plan (tabular)

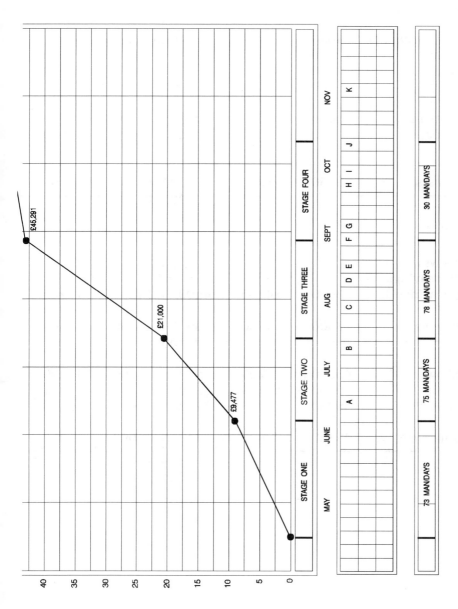

Figure 3.19 Graphical summary: PRINCE case study

	Year 0	Year 1	Year 2	Year 3	Year 4
Costs					
Staff – development	34000				
Hardware	12000				
Software	0				
Environment	100				
Running costs	100	200	200	200	200
Consumables	1000	500	500	500	500
Maintenance	250	500	500	500	500
Other					
Total costs	48350	1200	1200	1200	1200
Benefits					
Staff savings					
Accom. savings					
Other savings	3000	14400	14400	14400	14400
Total benefits	3000	14400	14400	14400	14400
Cashflow	-45350	13200	13200	13200	13200
Discount factor %	1.0000	0.9434	0.8900	0.8396	0.7921
Annual NPV	-45350	12453	11748	11083	10456
Cumulative NPV	-45350	-32897	-21149	-10066	389

Figure 3.20 Investment appraisal

4 | Project Initiation

Objectives

At the very beginning of a project (and we are talking about the first few days, the first 2–3 percent of the whole project), a Project Initiation Document should be produced. This is a major management control to ensure that the project starts off on a solid footing. Its objectives are to:

- formally initiate the project
- make sure that there is agreement between Project Board and Project Management on the objectives of the project
- define a total high-level plan for the project, giving a general idea of the timescale, when major events will occur, the resource and budget needs
- ensure that a reasonable business case exists before incurring more than minimal costs
- confirm the responsibilities and levels of authority of:
     the Project Manager
     the first Stage Manager (if this role is to be used)
     the members of the Project Assurance Team
     In practice it is also useful to confirm what the roles of
     the Project Board members entail. Often they have re-
     ceived no clear description of their role before they see
     the job description in the Project Initiation Document.
- indicate the level of quality to be achieved and the methods which will be used to ensure this
- plan the first stage of the project in detail and define the controls to be used in that plan
- ensure that all the pre-requisites for the project have been met

Project Initiation Activities

The preparation of the document is done by:

- the Project Manager
- the members of the Project Assurance Team
- the first Stage Manager (if the role is used)

The Project Initiation Meeting which will review the document should be called by the Executive as soon as possible after the IT Executive Committee has given approval for the project to proceed.

PRINCE defines the major activities as:

- confirming the Project Brief
- defining the project organisation
- creating an agreed plan for the overall project
- agreeing into how many stages the project will be broken
- producing a Business Case for the project
- Produce the first stage plans.

Preparation

The preparation of plans at the beginning of a project presents a number of problems:

- The preparation of the Project Plans may represent a considerable effort, and the Project Board may wish to review and approve them before the plans for the first stage are prepared. In fact, the number and position in the project of the stages may not be decided until the Project Plans have been completed. If this is so, it should be made clear in the initial brief given to the Project Manager.
- The Project Brief handed down by the IT Executive Committee may prove to be incomplete in some respects. The Project Manager may need to consult with the Project Board (and possibly other user managers as directed by the Project Board) to clarify and document the brief.
- Not all of the information required to be in the Project Initiation Document may be available in the first few days of the project.

The Project Initiation Meeting can take place with some information missing. It is usually better to do this than delay the meeting by any significant time. This still affords the Project Board the opportunity to review any problems and authorise a specific course of action. Such a meeting could:

- make as many decisions as it can with the information available
- approve as much of the Project Initiation Document as already exists, and record the actions necessary to complete assign responsibilities and resources needed to carry out those actions.

It may be possible to authorise a short first stage which concentrates on drawing up the complete set of plans required. Alternatively, a Mid-Stage Assessment could be held during the first stage to review and approve the completed plans.

Project Initiation Contents

Project Organisation Diagram

There should be a picture of at least the management structure of the project with actual names attached to the roles.

Job Descriptions
For each person identified in the organisation chart there should be a job description.

Project Brief
The Project Brief is handed to the Executive of the Project Board by the IT Executive Committee. It should contain:-
- a definition of the project
- the project Terms of Reference
- the scope and boundaries of the work, external interfaces and their frequencies, what is outside the project scope
- constraints; limiting factors on the solution, such as cost and schedule
- the overall tolerance levels to be allowed for the project without reference back to that committee.

Project Terms of Reference
The aims of the Terms of Reference are to:
- tell the Project Manager what the objectives of the project are
- identify the priorities within these objectives. If the project were to run into trouble at any time the Project Manager could then use these priorities to make the right decision on what to do. Once defined they should not change, otherwise the job of the Project Manager becomes impossible.

Business Case
The viability and justification of a project should be considered before major expenditure occurs. The Business Case has two parts, a Cost/Benefit Analysis to show what benefits and savings will the final product bring, measured against its cost, and an assessment of the Business Risks involved in undertaking the project.

Cost/Benefit Analysis

The analysis is divided into two sections. The first is costs. These are the estimated new system operating costs and development costs. The development costs can be taken from the Project Resource Plan. In Appendix D is a typical format for the collection of operating cost information, showing some of the headings under which operating costs can be quantified.

The second section covers an assessment of the benefits and savings to be gained by undertaking the project. In order to do this, the client must estimate the economic life of the product and be able to describe its benefits in monetary terms over the life span. The savings include present system operating costs plus resale or quantified residual value of the product or any of its components at the end of its operational life. Appendix D again contains a typical form for the collection of data on benefits and savings.

Both sets of figures are then adjusted in the forecast of future years in the table by the estimated rate of inflation. The main items of interest are the point at which the project starts showing a positive return and the overall return on the investment in the project.

Risk Management

The second part of the Business Case examines the risks being run by the project, the management, client, resources, all factors which will affect the performance of the project in order to assess what business risks are being taken. Each parameter is considered under two headings; how much risk is involved and how serious is that risk to the project. Figure 4.1 is a suggested Risk Management Checklist, provided by the CCTA, which is very easy to complete. Simple mathematics at the end give a crude guide to whether the project should be considered to be of high, medium or low risk. The use of this particular risk checklist is not mandatory. There are others on the market, or you can create your own. What is important is that an assessment of the risks is carried out before incurring large expenditure on the project. A proposal should be attached to the completed checklist, indicating where possible what action can be taken to avoid or lessen each of the high risks.

In Appendix D there is a list of standard activities carried out during Project Initiation.

Planning a Project

The Project Plan is an important management product input to this meeting. The major purposes of the Project Plan are to:

- input to the Business Case an estimate of how much the project development will cost
- input to the Project Initiation meeting an idea of how long the project will take.

Risk Management Checklist	Document No.	
Other Headings	Status	
Stage	Original Date	
Project Manager	Change Date	Version No.
Stage Manager	Author	

The risk factors, ie those factors which affect the probability that the project will be completed on time and within budget, and will deliver a quality product, come from four sources – project management, project staff, the nature of the project itself, and the maturity of the departmental management culture. These factors are itemised below, in the form of pairs of statements typifying low and high risk, on either side of a scale 1 to 4. one number in each of the scales is ringed to indicate my assessment of the risk attached to each factor. The ringed figure is multiplied by the weighting factor I have inserted in column (d) to give the figure in column (e).

(a) Low risk	(b) Scale	(c) High risk	(d) Weighting used (with suggested range)	(e) Total (bxd)
Project management				
1. Full time, experienced project manager	1 2 3 4	Inexperienced or part time project manager	___ (5–7)	___ *
2.. User management is experienced and likely to be active participators	1 2 3 4	inexperienced user management, with little participation expected	___ (4–6)	___ *
Project staff				
3. Users expected to be of good quality, actively involved, with relevant knowledge of the system	1 2 3 4	Little user involvement and little relevant knowledge expected	___ (3–5)	___ *
4. High standard of supervision and narrow span of control	1 2 3 4	Span of supervision too wide and level of control inadequate	___ (4–6)	___
5. The technical team is experienced, of good quality and with appropriate skills	1 2 3 4	Inexperienced team lacking the appropriate skills	___ (2[4)	___
6. Staff are dedicated to project	1 2 3 4	Staff have other responsibilities such as system maintenance	___ (3–5)	___
7. Low staff turnover	1 2 3 4	High staff turnover	___ (4–6)	___

Figure 4.1 Risk management checklist

(a) Low risk	(b) Scale	(c) High risk	(d) Weighting used (with sugeested range)	(e) Total (bxd)
The nature of the project				
8. Staff are experienced in quality reviews and committed to their use	1 2 3 4	No quality reviews carried out in the past	___ (4–6)	___
9. A typical system development cycle, with requirements definition, system specification, system design, etc.	1 2 3 4	A system development cycle having no formal definition, systems design and build merge, etc.	___ (2_4)	___
10. No unique or new features	1 2 3 4	Pioneering, new hardware or software, etc.	___ (2–4)	___
11. Current main operations will be affected minimally	1 2 3 4	Significant impact on mainstream operations	___ (3–5)	___
12. Hardware and software requirements determined and documents based on proven standards	1 2 3 4	Requirements not documented, or based on proven standards; limited safety margins for contingencies	___ (2–4)	___
13. Little or no modification to existing application software	1 2 3 4	Extensive modification needed	___ (2–5)	___
14. Little or no other development work being undertaken concurrently	1 2 3 4	Othe projects being developed concurrently	___ (2–5)	___
15. Little or no dependence on existing or developing systems not under the control of staff on this project	1 2 3 4	Dependent on other facilities not under the control of staff on this project	___ (3–6)	___
16. Project duration of one year or less, or small number of workdays compared with other completed projects	1 2 3 4	Project duration more than one year, or a large number of workdays	___ (2–4)	___
17. Little constraint on completion date beyond availablility of resources	1 2 3 4	Mandatory completion date	___ (3–5)	___
18. Plans and estimates are based on reliable data	1 2 3 4	Planning and estimation data are unreliable	___ (3–6)	___
19. Investment appraisal and estimates prepared and well documented, using proven standards	1 2 3 4	Approximations used or estimates not properly documented, or based on proven standards	___ (3–5)	___

Figure 4.1 (continued)

(a) Low risk	(b) Scale	(c) High risk	(d) Weighting used (with suggested range)	(e) Total (bxd)
20. Suppliers are large, well established companies	1 2 3 4	Suppliers are new or one-man businesses	___ (2–4)	___
21. Few user departments	1 2 3 4	Several user departments	___ (4–6)	___
22. The work affects few sites, which are easily accessible to the team	1 2 3 4	Many, or remote, sites are involved	___ (3–5)	___
The maturity of the departmental organisation				
24. A well developed set of standards is in use	1 2 3 4	Few standards are available	___ (2–4)	___
25. A well defined quality policy exists	1 2 3 4	The quality policy is ill defined	___ (3–5)	___
26 Clear delegation of authority is practised	1 2 3 4	Centralised management with little delegation	___ (2–4)	___
27. Good relationship with Departmental Trade Union Side and with staff	1 2 3 4	Relations with DTUS and staff are poor	___ (2–4)	___
28. Brought forward from continuation sheet (attached)			___	___
		Totals	___	___

High risk if greater than _____ (Total of column (d) x 2.6)
Low risk if less than _____ (Total of column (d) x 2.0)

(see note 1e on page 4)

My assessment of the risk of this project (see notes 1f & 2 on page 4) is

Very High _____   Acceptable _____)   Tick one
High   _____   Low   _____)

My recommendations for the risks identified by 3 or 4 marking against any of the above factors are attached (or in the Project Initiation Document if appropriate).

Signed _____   Date _____

(Project manager)

Figure 4.1 (continued)

Notes:
1. The assessment sheets should be completed as follows:

   a. Assess a weighting for each of the risk factors, and enter it in column (d). A recommended range is shown in brackets for each factor. Any weighting may be used, but the reason for any figure outside the recommended range should be recorded (see note 2 below).

   c. Multiply ringed number by the appropriate weighting, and enter the result in column (e).

   d. Assess whether there are any additional risks not included in this assessment sheet. If there are, enter them on a continuation sheet, and assess them as in 1a to 1c above. Total the continuation sheet and carry the totals onto page 3 of this checklist.

   e. Total the weighting factors in column (d). Multiply the resulting figure by 2.0 to obtain the low risk limit, and by 2.6 to obtain the high risk limit. Enter these two limits against "Low risk" and "High risk" respectively, on page 3.

   f. Total column (e) and enter the result on page 3.

   g. Assess the risk of the whole project, bearing in mind the spread of markings in column (b), any relevant departmental standards, and experience with other projects. **NB** The risk factors marked with an asterisk in column (e) are regarded as critical to the success of the project. If any of them receives a marking of 4 in column (b), or if 2 or more receive a marking of 3, the project must be assessed as high risk, or very high risk, whatever the total score may be.

2. Any areas of high risk within the project, the reasons for selecting any weighting factors which are outside the recommended range, and the overall assessment, should be recorded and itemised in the Project Initiation Document, along with recommendations about action to counter the risk, for approval by the Project Board. Thereafter, the degree of risk must be kept under review, to ensure that a low risk project does not become a high risk without the change being noticed. The risk should be reassessed before each End Stage Assessment (except the last one) is held, and reported to the Project Board as part of the request to commence the next stage. All changes to assessed risk from the previous submission must be pointed out and commented upon.

3. If the assessment indicates that the project has little or no chance of successful completion, the IT Executive committee must be informed (by the Project Board).

Figure 4.1 (continued)

Project Plan Format
The format will be exactly that described in the previous chapter, from Product Breakdown Structure to Technical and Resource Plans. Chapter 6 covers the detailed technique of creating a PRINCE plan.

Although it is a major input into the decision whether or not to undertake the project, it needs to be done quickly and before major expenditure on the project. Hence it is only a high-level plan. As a rough guide for an average project the plan should contain between 10 and 20 products.

It is not normal at this time to name the individual resources unless it is obvious at the outset that the project will require certain specific ones. It is usually sufficient to identify the type of resources, their cost and the approximate effort needed from each type.

Project Technical Plan
On the Technical Plan the columns might be in units of weeks, months or even longer if it is a very large project. We are not looking at this plan for precise detail. It is more useful to show the whole project on one form in weeks than show it in days over three forms.

In the previous chapter we mentioned another look at the management and quality products at this point to see if anything extra should be added to the activities. Make sure at this point that resources have been added to the Project Technical Plan to carry out the Quality Reviews and Checkpoint Meetings, update plans, report to the Project Board and prepare for the End-Stage Assessment.

Project Resource Plan
Figure 4.2 reminds us of the Resource Plan for our example in Chapter 3. Although we didn't mention this at the time, this is a Project Resource Plan. The effort and costs have been summarised into stages. Later in this chapter we shall look at dividing a project into stages.

Project Quality Plan
As part of our Plan Description we need to add information on how we intend to achieve and ensure a quality product. This has several parts.
- The first statement should cover our quality policy. Consider the difference in the quality of products which will result from a policy of 'If it isn't perfection, it isn't good enough' compared to 'If it works, it'll do'. Is there a company policy? What is your policy with regard to the quality of the products (both final and interim products!)? If the client has laid down any specific quality demands, these should be repeated here. They may include Mean Time Between Failure (MTBF) or Mean Time To Repair (MTTR). We should make sure that we get the client to define the priorities between time, cost and quality. If quality will

Effort	Stage 1	Stage 2	Stage 3	Stage 4
Ken Harper	1.75	1.25	3	0
Assistant	0.25	0.5	1.25	1.35
Total effort	2.00	1.75	4.35	1.25

Costs	£	£	£	£
Ken Harper	350	250	600	0
Assistant	25	50	125	125
Computer	10			
Sub-Total	385	300	725	125
Printing		25		
Development		25		
Materials		20		
Stamps/env		100		
Total	385	300	915	125
Cumulative	385	685	1600	1725

Figure 4.2 Project resource plan

take a little longer or cost a little more, is the client prepared to pay
for it? Is the final product to be used once and then thrown away?
This happened quite often when we handled the program demands of
the exploration side of an oil company. In this case the quality of screen
presentation and user guides were usually less important than speed
of delivery.

- There must then be a paragraph stating our quality strategy, how we
intend to meet the quality policy statement, the general means we will
use to achieve and ensure quality. What equipment, techniques,
production methods will we use to have a good chance of creating good
quality products? What methods, checklists and procedures will we
use to inspect the products for quality? Are there specific moments in
the project when quality inspection will be carried out? In PRINCE
terms, this means identifying the major project products which will
be subject to Quality Reviews, specific inspections by those with a
vested interest in the completeness and accuracy of the product.
- The Product Descriptions mentioned in the previous chapter also form
part of the Quality Plan.

Configuration Management Plan
Another addition to the Plan Description in our Project Plan is an expla-

nation of how we intend to control and keep track of the finished products. There would normally be a reference to the project organisation, to indicate who would be taking on the role of Configuration Librarian. This is dealt with in detail in the chapter on Configuration Management, 'Controlling the Products'.

Dividing a Project into Stages

As has already been mentioned, the Project Plan is a high-level view of the total job, which does not try to go into detail. We need a method of breaking the project down into parts which can be planned in detail in order to exercise any control.

Firstly, let us remind ourselves of the reasons for breaking projects into stages. There are reasons from the point of view of the Project Manager and different ones seen by the Project Board.

The Project Manager

1. In order to exercise control against a plan, that plan must be in such detail that every activity will only take a few days. PRINCE suggests ten days as a maximum. Five or less would be even better for the purposes of control. If you give a resource three days to do a small job, at the very worst you know after three days if there is to be any slippage. If you don't break the work down sufficiently and you give a resource, say, four weeks to do a job, let's have a look at what is likely to happen. After five days, if nothing disastrous has happened, the resource will report back either that the work is on schedule or, with human nature's natural optimism, ahead of schedule. If a problem arises, the resource will either believe that this has been allowed for in the estimate, and therefore there is no slippage, or will believe that a breakthrough is just around the corner, and so will still report that progress is on schedule. The resource will be convinced that things will turn out right until time runs out and the truth has to be admitted. Most of us experience this time and time again with the chores we plan to do around the house. So there you are, three weeks have gone by and you find out that there is going to be slippage too late normally for you to do anything about it. Had you broken that work into three or more pieces, you would have been able to react much earlier. Also if you had split the work up, you and the resource would have had a better idea on whether the deadlines were achievable in the first place.
2. For any project you can visualise the next few activities quite clearly, but the further you go into the future, the more vague it gets, the more unknowns come into play. The Stage Plan is going to be the Project Manager's commitment, so it makes sense to limit it to as far ahead as can be seen comfortably.
3. It would take an enormous amount of time to sit down and plan a long

period of time ahead in the kind of detail which will make control possible. If you add to this the fact that the further you go into the future, the less accurate you are likely to be, it makes sense to take a small amount of time and plan only a short stretch ahead.

Project Board

1. One way to limit the size of risk being taken with a project is not to commit everything at the outset, but to commit a small amount of the resources, check if you like the results of that piece of work, then commit the next small chunk. One of the principal reasons for breaking a project down into stages is to allow the Project Board to limit the size of risk it is taking at any one time. The commitment from them is only one stage at a time, just as it is for the Project Manager.

2. A very good way of keeping tabs on Project Managers is to make sure they have to come back to the Project Board at regular intervals for funds to continue the project. These are ideal moments to find out the state of the project so far and what is planned for the next period ahead.

So there we are, the major reasons for breaking a project into stages:

- not too long spent in planning at any one time
- a detailed plan is produced against which reasonable control can be exercised
- commitment is against a detailed plan
- the amount of project budget to be risked at any time can be controlled
- it provides an ideal management control point at the end of one stage and the beginning of the next when the Project Manager has to meet and report to the Project Board.

The first stage in a PRINCE project is normally very small. It may only cover the work necessary to produce the Project Initiation Document. The reason goes back to what we have just said about risk. The Project Initiation Document contains information on whether a good business case exists for the project and what business risks are to be faced. So the Project Board want to have a look at this information before authorising the project to continue.

A sensible moment at which to consider into what stages a project should be broken is after production of the Project Technical Plan. Here we can see the main events of the project against a timeframe. We can see when important products will be finished. In PRINCE a stage will always be marked by the delivery of one or more of the major products.

Going back to our Christmas card example, Figure 4.3 shows a possible division of the project into four stages. The PRINCE symbol for a stage division is a cross within a circle, as can be seen at the bottom of the form. This would end stages on:

- the production of the Project Initiation Document

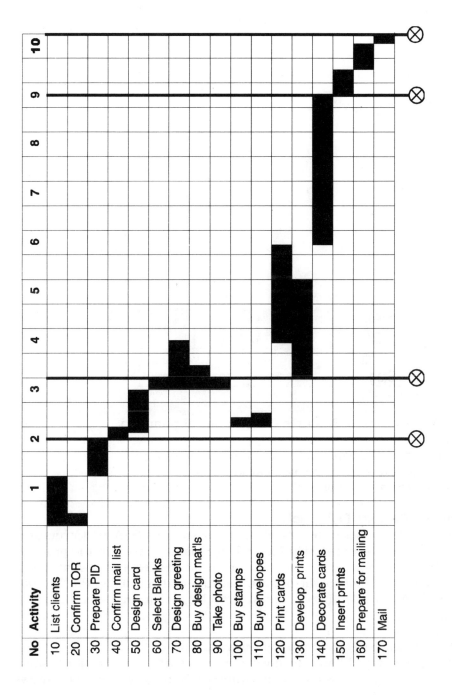

Figure 4.3 Possible Project Stage Divisions

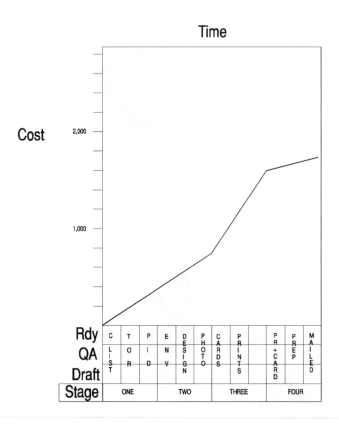

Figure 4.4 Project Resource Plan Graphical Summary

- delivery of the card design and the staff photo
- production of the decorated cards
- completion of the project

Imposed Project Life Cycle

It may be that a set of technical methods such as SSADM (Structured Systems Analysis and Design Methodology) is to be used in the projects. SSADM has its own stages, timed to occur on the delivery of what it sees as the major products of the project. Because of its flexibility PRINCE has no problems in adapting to the stage selection of any such technical methodology.

Project Resource Plan Graphical Summary

Now that the project has been divided into its stages, we are in a position to produce a Project Resource Plan Graphical Summary. Figure 4.4 shows one for our example project.

Tolerance

It is not humanly possible to be one hundred percent accurate with a plan. But PRINCE says that if a project plan deviates from the expected, the Project Board must refer the project back to the IT Executive Committee for a decision on whether to continue. So if the plan is a day out or ten pounds over budget, is this a deviation? Clearly some common sense is called for. When the IT Executive Committee passes down a project to a Project Board it should indicate an expected cost and target schedule (probably taken from an earlier Feasibility Study) and a margin on either side of these figures within which actual completion will be acceptable. This margin is called the Tolerance level. It is usually expressed as a percentage of the total, and usually the same figure applies to the budget and the schedule.

A note describing what the Tolerance level is for the project should be included in the Plan Description. As progress is made through the project, the Project Plan will be updated in the light of better information. This must be checked to ensure that the updated Project Plan still stays within the overall Tolerance. Otherwise, as perviously stated, the Executive has to go back to the IT Executive Committee for direction.

Figure 4.4 shows a Resource Graph for our Christmas Card project. The solid line shows the project cost rising through the selected number of stages to 1725. The dotted lines on either side show a Tolerance corridor of 20%. As long as the actuals stay within the corridor as the project progresses, it is regarded as being within tolerance and need not be referred back to the IT Executive Committee. The actuals line shows that we have completed stages 1 and 2. Although the project exceeded its forecast budget for stage 1, it stayed within the tolerance allowed. By the end of stage 2 the cumulative cost has fallen below the planned figure, but is again within the tolerance corridor.

Having had a tolerance level defined for the entire project, this becomes a constraint on the tolerance level which can be allowed for any stage plan within the project. The approach to the setting of tolerances for a stage plan is discussed in a later section of this chapter, 'Planning a Stage'.

Maintaining the Project File

The Project File is established in the first stage of a project. It is the responsibility of the Project Manager, but often delegated to the Business Assurance Co-ordinator. It should contain three sections:

> *Organisation*
> A copy of the organisation diagram, agreed job descriptions and reporting structure should be kept here.

Plans

The Project Plans should be kept here. They should be updated at the end of each stage with information on the actuals. Any modification to the Project Plans should be put onto new versions of the plan. The original ones agreed at Project Initiation should always be kept unchanged to show the picture at the project outset.

Controls

All the Project Board Approvals from each End-Stage Assessment should be filed here, together with any Mid-Stage Assessment Approvals. A copy of the Project Initiation Document, the meeting to approve it, copies of the various Highlight Reports and Acceptance Letters, and minutes of the Project Closure meeting are also filed here.

Planning a Stage

A Stage Plan is an extract of the part of the Project Plan. It will be planned in much more detail than the Project Plan, will name the specific resources to be used and allocate these to their respective activities.

It is recommended that the creation of a Stage Plan follows exactly the same steps as the Project Plan:

- *Stage Product Breakdown Structure* – The first step in producing the plan is to extract from the project Product Breakdown Structure those products which will be delivered during the stage. These are then broken down to their sub-products. This continues until each sub-product will only take a small number of days to produce. These sub-products require Product Descriptions to be written about them.
- *Stage Product Flow Diagram* – a diagram of the products to be produced during the stage, showing the sequence of their production and from which other products they are derived.
- *Stage Activity Network* – a network showing the activities necessary to produce the products plus the relationships and dependencies between them.
- *Stage Technical Plan* – normally a Bar Chart. It displays the technical activities and allocated resources against an appropriate timescale, and identifies the frequency and timing of Checkpoint Meetings, Quality Reviews and any Mid-Stage Assessments.
- *Stage Resource Plan* – a tabular view of the resource needs and costs of the Stage Technical Plan. The PRINCE manuals suggest that the requirements are summarised in columns of one month or week. When considering which to use, it is sensible to think of a unit of time which corresponds to the Project Board's request for a Highlight

Report, then it is easy to show actuals against plan. The agreed tolerance level for the stage should also be shown on this plan in terms of cost and timescale.

- *Stage Resource Plan Graphical Summary* – a graph with time and cost axes with a line showing the accumulating costs over the duration of the stage. For a Stage Plan the time columns should reflect a suitable time period according to the total duration of the plan, typically a week. A good idea is to show with a different type of line or colour the tolerance margins on each side of the planned line.
- *Stage Plan Description* – text describing what the plan is, any relevant background, the approach taken, plus any pre-requisites, assumptions and risks. If there have been any major changes to the Terms of Reference since the previous stage, such as Requests For Change or Off-Specifications with a large impact on cost, schedule, priorities, approach or quality strategy, this should be stated here. The stage tolerance should be agreed between Project Manager and Project Board and identified here, plus the reporting requirements.
- *Stage Quality Plan* – as part of the Plan Description, this should identify any types of test to be carried out during the stage and any formal Quality Reviews. The effort for these must be shown in the Stage Technical Plan. If possible, all the resources for each Quality Review should be identified, but minimally the Chairman of each review should be shown. The Stage Quality Plan should also contain Product Descriptions for the more detailed products identified as being produced in the stage.

The last five of these, Stage Technical Plan, Resource Plan, Resource Graphical Summary, Plan Description and Stage Quality Plan are mandatory. The others form recommended support documents.

Example

Let's go back to the Christmas card project and look at the production of one of the stage plans. Of course, we're dealing with a very short time span, but it will serve to give an idea of the approach. Figure 4.3 reminds us of the selected stages in our project. Our example takes the second stage, after the presentation of the Project Initiation Document.

The products to be completed in the stage are:

- an approved card design
- a confirmed mailing list
- the selection of a blank card on which the Christmas card is to be produced
- the greeting to go in the card
- the materials to decorate the cards
- the staff photograph to go on the front of the Christmas card

Let's have a look at how the last one of these, the staff photograph, might be broken down. Our first pass at a breakdown might look like this:

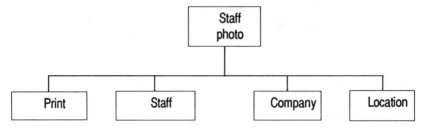

Thinking back on how we obtain the Print we might come up with the further breakdown of:

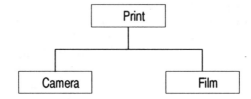

And so the gradual breakdown of the products might continue. At the next step the Product Flow Diagram might look like Figure 4.5.

Adding the activities to this diagram might leave us with a list like the following. They are summarised under the Project Plan activity numbers just to help you follow the breakdown.

> 40 Confirm mail list
>> 10 Check list with sales rep
>> 20 Telephone to confirm doubtful contact names
>> 30 Update list
> 50 Design card
>> 10 Meeting to establish Managing Director's views
>> 20 Design general layout
>> 30 Produce three designs
>> 40 Meeting to select design
> 60 Select card blanks
>> 10 Identify required dimensions from design
>> 20 Confirm numbers required
>> 30 Visit printer & identify available options
>> 40 Examine options & select card
> 70 Design greeting
>> 10 Identify theme from card design
>> 20 Write four proposed greetings

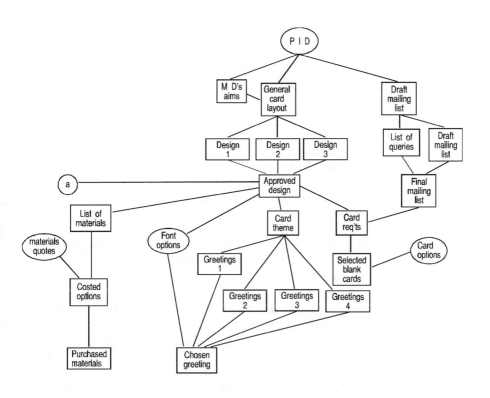

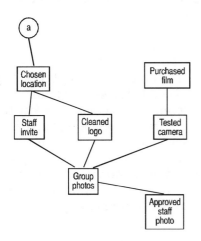

Figure 4.5 Stage PFD

              30 Select font type and size
              40 Meeting to choose greeting
       80 Buy design materials
              10 List desired materials and quantity
              20 Obtain two prices and select vendor
              30 Purchase materials
       90 Take Photo
              10 Check camera
              20 Obtain film
              30 Take test film
              40 Decide location
              50 Ensure company logo clean
              60 Arrange for staff to be present
              70 Assemble staff and take one dozen photos

At this level of detail, differences might appear between the Stage Plan and the less detailed Project Plan. For example, it may now seem that activity 90 (Take photo) cannot be accomplished within the half day originally estimated. Other activities may take more or less time. Experience shows that as an activity is studied in more detail, it is usually revealed that it will need more rather than less time. This is one reason for the Tolerance margin. The Project Manager now has to decide whether the plan can be accomplished within the overall tolerances or not. In the example activity we have taken, we could no doubt overlap some of the earlier sub-activities of 'Take photo' with other things. But what about cost? Considerations such as these and the agreement on them which has to be reached with the Project Board in order to get their approval demonstrate how sensible it is to plan in stages and get clearance from the management every step of the way.

Detailed Plans

Detailed Plans are optional but may be required in some stages. They comprise a Detailed Technical Plan and a Detailed Resource Plan.

A Detailed Technical Plan gives greater detail about a major activity than might be desired in the Stage Technical Plan from which it is derived. It is used to control staff working on particular activities. For example, in a project to develop a computer system a Detailed Technical Plan could be prepared to control system testing or the data conversion activity. It is matched by the Detailed Resource Plan. An accurate summary of both must be shown in the Stage Technical and Resource Plans.

Individual Work Plans

Individual Work Plans are used to assign technical activities to individual team members. They will be derived directly from the Stage Technical Plan or the Detailed Technical Plan and will form the basis for discussion of progress at the regular Checkpoint Meetings. They often comprise an extract from the higher level bar chart. It is sensible to restrict the extract to the next few activities looking about one month ahead. This gives the Stage or Project Manager flexibility if resources need to be changed around. The Individual Work Plan should be accompanied by any relevant Product Descriptions and sufficient extra documentation that the team member knows how successful completion will be measured. This should include any Quality Review requirements for the product(s) to be developed, indications as to whether these should be formal or informal, and an indication of any specific resources which should be invited to the review.

As each Individual Work Plan is completed, the Stage or Project Manager should assess the performance of the team member on the allocated tasks and discuss that appraisal with the individual. The meeting should be documented, and will form the basis of any annual assessment of that person's work plus their training needs.

Stage Management Activities
In Appendix D there is a list of the standard activities which are carried out by the management team and Project Assurance Team in any stage.

5 | Monitoring and Reporting

The Purpose of Control

The purpose of the PRINCE control structure is to ensure that the project maintains its:

- *business integrity* – that is it is on schedule and in accordance with its planned budget
- *technical integrity* – that the system Products being produced meet the required specification, performance and reliability standards and that the final delivered system will be maintainable.

Controls are necessary to ensure that, for each level of the project organisation, the higher level of management can:

- monitor progress
- compare achievement with plan
- detect problems
- initiate corrective action

A major function of the Project Assurance Team is to assist project management in monitoring and reporting progress. This chapter looks at Checkpoint Meetings and Highlight Reports, two regularly occurring elements of control in which they assist the Stage and Project Manager to communicate stage progress up to Project Board level.

Exercise of Control

Control is exercised by comparing actual achievement against planned achievement. The aim is to detect departures from plan as early as possible and to take the required action to bring the project back on course. These departures from plan include any problems in the quality of products. PRINCE requires action to be taken on any deviation from plan which is outside the allowed and agreed tolerances. Tolerances can be either Management Tolerances or Technical Tolerances.

Management Tolerances – a percentage deviation on the plan cost or schedule. It is agreed between the Project Board and the Project Manager at the End Stage Assessment meeting which initiates the stage. The Project Board have to bear in mind the overall tolerance levels for the project which were handed down from the IT Executive Committee, while the Project Manager will be looking at the number of uncertainties in the plan. As a practical guide this should never be less than ten percent, even for a small stage where everything is well known and has been done many times. A more normal figure would be twenty percent, and higher for research-type work where there are more unknowns than knowns ahead.

Technical Tolerances – tolerances on the performance or quality of products. It is defined in the User Acceptance Criteria, which are taken from the User Requirements and objectives.

Checkpoint Meetings
Checkpoints are internal progress meetings. Checkpoint Meetings are held on a regular, time related basis, usually weekly. The frequency of them is agreed at the previous End-Stage Assessment.

Objectives
- To review progress against Individual Work Plans and record actual resource usage
- to identify when Individual Work Plans need refreshing
- to exchange information about progress and problems across the team(s)
- to disseminate downwards any information from the Project Board, department and Project Manager
- to provide the input to the Checkpoint Reports to the Project Manager, which will provide the basis for Highlight Reports from the Project Manager to the Project Board

Participants
Checkpoint Meetings are held at team level. PRINCE suggests that they are run by the Stage Manager or a member of the Project Assurance Team. If the Stage Manager role is not being used, a Team Leader may conduct the meeting. It is always useful if at least one member of the Project Assurance Team does attend in order to keep abreast of progress and problems.

Meeting Conduct
At the meeting team members provide details of the work and achievements since the last Checkpoint Meeting. This information is written up on a Checkpoint Meeting Report normally by the Business Assurance Co-ordinator. If the project is so large that there is more than one team, they may all attend one meeting or each team have a Checkpoint meeting of its own. The decision here is a balance of the advantage of face-to-face news exchange and the inefficiency of large meetings (plus the question of team work locations).

The meeting is also used to identify any necessary updates to Individual

Work Plans. If a software package is being used to capture actual work effort, the time sheets can be collected either at the Checkpoint Meeting or separately.

Activities
Preparation

1. Confirm data and time of Checkpoint	Stage Manager
2. Complete weekly timesheet	Team members
3. Identify products completed	Team Leader
4. Identify any activity slippage and revise remaining effort and target date.	Team member

Review

1. Compare work done with work planned	All
2. Review resource usage against plan	All
3. Identify and quantify all problems	All
4. Agree solutions for problems where possible.	All
5. Decide action where solution cannot be agreed	All
6. Check for any requirements for update-sagreed to Individual Work Plans	Stage Manager
7. Disseminate any news from higher management levelsStage Manager	Stage Manager

Follow-Up

1. Ensure that the Stage Technical Plan is updated with actuals	TAC
2. Ensure that the Stage Resource Plan is updated with actuals	BAC
3. Prepare any new Individual Work Plans	Stage Manager
4. Prepare Checkpoint Report	BAC

Highlight Reports
The Highlight Report is a regular summary of the Stage progress for the Project Board. It reviews progress to date, highlights actual or potential problems and forecasts progress for the next period. The frequency is normally monthly, but determined by the Project Board at the previous End-Stage Assessment.

The responsibility for its delivery to the Project Board lies with the Project Manager. It is normally prepared by the Business Assurance Co-ordinator from the Checkpoint Reports.

Highlight Report Activities

1. Check date report is due	Project Manager
2. Collect Checkpoint Reports	BAC
3. Check on status of any reported problems	Project Manager/BAC

4. Ensure Stage Technical and Resource Plans   BAC
   are up-to-date
5. Prepare report under Highlight Report form   Project Manager/BAC
   headings

Highlight Report Product Description
The PRINCE manual does not provide actual forms, but does give Product
Descriptions of them. This is the description in the PRINCE manual. If
busy senior management are going to read it, it should be as brief as
possible. It is recommended that the Highlight Report itself covers no more
than one page. In practice the information about budget and schedule can
be given by attaching a copy of either the Stage Resource Plan or Stage
Resource Plan Graphical Summary.

Purpose
To provide the Project Board, at pre-defined points, with a brief summary
of the project status.

Contents
Reporting period – work period covered by the report.
Date due – planned delivery date of this report.
Budget status:-
        planned expenditure during the period
        actual expenditure during the period
Deviation
        planned total expenditure to date
        actual total expenditure to date
        deviation.
Exceptions
        activities planned to start but not started
        activities started but not planned
        activities planned to finish but not finished.
Highlights
        a summary of the major events (achievements and fail-
        ures) of the reporting period. In terms of achievements
        it is easiest to concentrate on products delivered, how-
        ever small these may have been. The section should
        relate to those items listed to be complete in the 'outlook'
        section of the previous report.
Potential Problems
        any actual or potential problems. For potential problems
        there should be a proposal of any action which can be
        reasonably taken to prevent or reduce the problem.

Outlook
>   a forecast of the stage progress over the next period. This should include a list of all products to be completed in the period, however small.

Signature
>   Project Manager's signature and date.

6 | Controlling the Products

The Meaning of Configuration

A configuration is a logically related set of products which need to be managed as a composite set. In PRINCE the term means the sum total of technical products which comprise the final delivered system.

These products are called *Configuration Items*. For a computer system they will be, for example, the object code and initial files. Among these products will also be documentation such as user manuals and training materials.

In order to understand the PRINCE concept of Configuration Management it is important to differentiate between a Configuration Item and an interim technical product. If it is a technical product which will be required to operate or maintain the final system, then it is a Configuration Item. Otherwise PRINCE refers to everything else as a product.

Configuration Item Life Cycles

Work to develop a Configuration Item may be carried out over more than one stage of the project. Within a stage there will be a number of steps defined which will either create the Configuration Item or change it from its present state to a new state. It is normal for an item to be at a specific, forecastable and usable position at the end of a stage.

All the stages in which work is carried out on the item and all the relevant steps within those stages form the life cycle of that Configuration Item. This life cycle has to be recorded on a form called the *Configuration Item Description Record*, together with information about any interim products which contribute to it at any point in the life cycle. Every item has its own description record. The content of this is defined later in the chapter.

Configuration Management

This is the name given to the monitoring and control of Configuration Items. Because the interim technical products are to be used to develop Configuration Items, Configuration Management needs to track them as well. Configuration Management provides techniques and procedures to perform the following functions:

- Identifying the individual Configuration Items which are to be man-

aged.
- Recording, monitoring and reporting on the current status of each Configuration Item as its development progresses through its own specific development life-cycle.
- Filing all development documentation produced during the development life of the Configuration Items.
- Distributing and recording holders of copies of all Configuration Items.
- Managing Project Issues raised during the project.
- Managing change to all Configuration Items, from the recording of Requests for Change, through assessment of the impact of proposed changes, release of both documentation and machine readable representations of the items, to the eventual receipt of the amended representations.
- Producing one or more release packages consisting of all the Configuration Items required to install the system. In order to do this, the method must be able to identify the appropriate version numbers of each Configuration Item which constitute a particular release.
- Being able to recreate any past release level of the system.

Configuration Management Responsibilities of Other Roles

Project Board
It is the responsibility of the Project Board to ensure that there is a Configuration Management Plan. It should be part of the Project Initiation Document submitted to them. The Project Board also have to satisfy themselves that there is an adequate resource allocation in the plans to implement the Configuration Librarian's job fully.

Project Manager
Although the day-to-day work will be done by the Configuration Librarian's role, it remains the overall responsibility of the Project Manager. The Project Manager is the one to ensure that a Configuration Management Plan forms part of the Project Initiation Document and that it has been resourced.

Approval of the identification scheme for Configuration Items and confirmation that the necessary Configuration Item Description Records have been created also rests with the Project Manager.

In addition, the Project Manager should ensure that Configuration Audit reports are prepared before Mid- and End-Stage Assessments.

Project Assurance Team
The Project Assurance Team review all Project Issues with the Stage Manager on their receipt from the Librarian and advise the Project

Manager on action.

If in the opinion of the Project Assurance Team a Project Issue is to become a Request For Change, each member must carry out an impact analysis, based at the outset on the information from the Configuration Item Description Records.

The Business Assurance Co-ordinator role has the responsibility for carrying out Configuration Audits with the Librarian.

Project Team Member
Team members have no specific Configuration Management roles. It is important that they obtain product copies only from the Configuration Librarian, and that they follow the correct procedures for submitting products and raising Project Issues.

Configuration Management Plan
This should be produced as part of the Project Initiation Document. Apart from the work during the project, it must be remembered that it will be necessary to continue Configuration Management throughout the life of the system. This means that the Configuration Management Method chosen should be transferable to the maintenance team at the end of the project. On a site with many systems under development it makes sense to seek a method common to all of them and to consider centralising the Configuration Librarian's job as part of a Project Support Office.

PRINCE recommends the following headings for the Configuration Management Plan.

Synopsis
For those unused to the Configuration Management concept, this introduces it and points out any variance in the methods to be used from site standards, and justifies the variance. For example, if some Configuration Items are to be bought in from a software house, the identification system, submission and issue procedures would be different.

Purpose
This identifies the system to be developed plus any links with the Configuration Management Plans of other projects. The purpose of the plan should describe the different types of product which it has to bring together and control.

Scope
If variations of the final system have to be produced, for example, to operate under different operating systems, to work on different computers, this would be described here. This section also defines which items will be

managed and which are outside the scope of the plan. An example here might be that the system will use modules common to other systems which are controlled by a different Configuration Management Method.

References
A list of standards to be used by products controlled by the Configuration Management Method should be provided.

Definitions and Abbreviations
This is like a glossary of terms. Any Configuration Management jargon, initials or names should be explained. The PRINCE manual suggests that only new terms need be covered, not those already covered in department standards. This depends on whether readers such as the Project Board will have ever seen these departmental standards. The best idea is to keep jargon down to a minimum and explain in this section all the special terms used.

Responsibilities
This is best done as a matrix, linking all Configuration Management activities with the role responsible.

Interfaces
This section identifies other methods, projects or external organisations with which the Configuration Management Method will have to interface. The PRINCE manual suggests that it should go down to the level of identifying modules or programs from outside sources which the project intends to use. At the Initiation stage this detailed information may not be available.

Filing
This is a very important section. It should define in detail the media, libraries and filing structure to be used to keep the various categories of Configuration Items. The categories cover hardware, software, documentation, human readable and machine readable items. If a computer-based Configuration Management tool is to be used, it should be identified here.

Document Issue Procedures
This section describes the procedures to be used to issue and distribute copies of managed documents. It is quite interesting that the PRINCE manual does not also suggest sections describing the issue of non-documents, such as machine readable products, or procedures for the submission of items to the Configuration Management Method. These would seem to be useful additions. The producer of the plan might feel

that these sections, together with the one covering document issue and the final one on Configuration Item identification might simply contain a reference to the procedures in the Configuration Management Plan presented to the Project Board, with the actual procedures held either as an appendix or by the Configuration Librarian.

Security
This section should define the physical and logical access security measures to be adopted for Configuration Items.

Configuration Item Identification
This section should define the naming and numbering conventions to be adopted for the various types of Configuration Item for this project. If it is to be a convention common to all systems on the site, it should still identify any prefix allocated to items from this project.

Configuration Management Structure and Identification Scheme
The idea of the structure is like a Bill of Material. You need to be able to identify the sub-assemblies and all their component parts which make up the total system. Getting this right is a difficult task, because there are so many interconnections and different views.

The first view is relatively simple and can be document-based. This is a view of all the Configuration Items which make up the final system viewed hierarchically, starting with the system at the top and decomposing this in the lower levels into its components. The PRINCE manual offers Product Breakdown Structures of a typical computer system, and some of those showing the Technical Products can be used as a basis to create the hierarchical Configuration Management structure.

PRINCE says that in the beginning the only Configuration Item which can be identified is the complete system itself. Only when the design has been agreed can lower level components begin to be identified.

The first complication comes because some of the low level items are machine readable products rather than human readable. The naming conventions for object decks held in computer libraries are usually constrained by the software, and our Configuration Management identification scheme needs to be able to associate the computer label with an identifier from its own scheme.

The next challenge is if modules common to other systems are used. Again the Configuration Management Method needs to define the naming conventions, structure and procedures to map such items to its particular system and control any changes to them.

Another problem is that Configuration Items change and develop. Our identifier needs to be able to pick up an item at any stage or step of its development. If different versions are produced, these too have to be tracked. Our structure becomes more like a multi-layered network. From the system level we have to be able to identify all the components and the specific stage and version number of each of them which link to a specific version of the system. For example, version 3.1 of our system might require version 6 of module abc and version 8 of module xyz. The changes made to module xyz mean that we must use version 3 of chapter 5 of the user manual, and so on. Every change to one module has a knock-on effect elsewhere in the structure. This leads us neatly to consider the information we need to store for each Configuration Item.

Configuration Item Description Record
The following information is needed to identify an item and enable the Configuration Management Method to track it through its various changes and link it in its correct position in the final system.
- Unique Identifier
- Description
- Life Cycle Description
- List of Parent Configuration Item
- List of Child Configuration Items
- Member of Staff Responsible
- Date from which responsible
- Source (e.g. in-house, bought in from company x)
- Current life cycle stage
- Current life cycle step
- Latest Baseline identity
- List of products required for this step
    product
    version number
    member of staff responsible
    date due
    date received
    list of reviewers
- Change History

Those readers with any experience of databases will appreciate that a lot of this information may be duplicated, so a link to where the data can be found, rather than a copy of the data would suffice.

Baselines
The above list used the word 'baseline' which is a key to Configuration Management. What does it mean?

A baseline is a snapshot of the state of a Configuration Item and its components at a point in time. The baseline identity consists of the identifier of the Configuration Item, the step, stage and version number. The same information is needed of its components.

The first baseline for a Configuration Item is established when the specification of the item has been quality reviewed and agreed. Subsequent baselines are established at points where the Configuration Item has been changed and is ready to be either used as a basis for further work or released as part of the working system.

A baseline can only be established when all products associated with the step and stage have been successfully quality reviewed. Every time a baseline is created, a new Configuration Item Description Record should be made out. The old one should be archived, because it must remain possible to recreate any baseline.

Configuration Control

The Configuration Management Method must contain procedures to control the submission and issue of Configuration Items. It would be sensible if these procedures also covered technical products on which the Configuration Items are built. The procedures must cater for machine readable as well as human readable items.

The Configuration Librarian is responsible for two types of documentation:

- the content of the Configuration Item itself
- information about the status of Configuration Items.

Submission Procedures

A product should be submitted to the Configuration Librarian only when the author is satisfied that it is ready for review. If you recall the Resource Plan Graphical Summary with the boxes at the bottom to indicate product status, this is the moment when the 'draft' box for the product could be ticked.

A Submission Request Form should accompany the product, detailing:

- what the document is
- submission date
- to which Configuration Item it relates
- the step and stage number in the Configuration Item's life cycle
- any necessary version number
- indication of any sensitivity or security classification
- name of the person submitting the product
- a list of the people who will attend its quality review

This final piece of information allows the Configuration Librarian to make copies for distribution to the Quality Review attendees.

Before accepting a product the Configuration Librarian must confirm that the product appears on a Configuration Item Description Record.

The actual procedure for accepting machine readable products will vary in detail depending on the hardware and software environment, but it should follow the same general lines. The Document Submission Form should still be used.

Issue Procedures

Master copies of baselined Configuration Items should always be retained by the Configuration Librarian and never issued. The librarian is responsible for maintaining an issue log for each Configuration Item to record:

- the identity and version of products issued
- the recipient's name
- the purpose of the issue
- the authority for the issue
- the date of issue

All officially issued document copies should be identified as such. They should be identified in a way that differentiates them from the master copy and also in such a way that differentiates them from unofficial copies. This can be achieved by numbering the official copies and using coloured paper for them. The purpose is to spot unofficial copies which are outside Configuration control and therefore may be obsolete or contain different information. Any work based upon such documents would run the risk of causing errors.

When an approved amendment to a controlled document is accepted into the library, all current copy holders should be notified, the obsolete versions withdrawn, destroyed and this fact recorded on the Configuration log. Copies of the new version are issued as required.

When the Project Manager approves a Request For Change the Configuration Librarian issues a copy of the current master document to the person allocated to do the work. The Configuration Management Method has to ensure that no document is on issue to more than one person at a time for the purpose of changing it.

Impact Analysis

This is another term used in Configuration Management. It is associated with the evaluation of Project Issues. These are examined by the Stage Manager (if this role is used) and Project Assurance Team. Where they are going to recommend that the issue is turned into either a Request For Change or an Off-Specification they have to provide an assessment of the work which would be involved.

The Technical Assurance Co-ordinator identifies which initial product is the subject of the issue. Then from an examination of the Configuration Item Description Records the librarian advises on which other products and Configuration Items would be affected. The Technical Assurance Co-ordinator analyses the work effort of any necessary changes and the Business Assurance Co-ordinator translates this into cost. This is Impact Analysis.

Configuration Status Accounting
A Configuration Status Accounting Report is produced by the Configuration Librarian for every Mid- and End-Stage Assessment. It takes all the Configuration Item Description Records which contain steps to be done during that stage and identifies:
- the status of the Configuration Item
- the current baseline identity
- which steps have been done
- the current step
- the status of all contributing products

The Configuration Librarian is also responsible for the control of Technical Exception documentation. From this the librarian is required to produce regular and ad-hoc reports on them, such as:
- the numbers of each type received:
    since the project began
    by stage
    within a specified period
- the numbers of each type closed:
    since the project began
    by stage
    within a specified period
- the implementation status of those where action has been approved
- a league table of the numbers of each type still unallocated by age

Configuration Audits
Configuration Audits are inspections of the Configuration Item Description Records and the latest version of the Configuration Item held in its development folder to ensure that:
- the documentation is up-to-date
- the item matches its specification
- the specification of each item is consistent with that of its parent
- standards are being met

The audits are usually carried out for each End-Stage Assessment. They are the responsibility of the Business Assurance Co-ordinator. If the Business Assurance Co-ordinator is also acting as the Configuration Librarian for the project, the Project Manager must appoint someone else to do the audit.

Management Configuration Items
PRINCE suggests that management products such as plans can be brought under greater control and discipline by making them Configuration Items and lodging them with the librarian. Against this idea is the fact that Configuration Management is difficult enough with just the technical products to worry about.

Desirable Configuration Management Method Features
When examining any offered solution or proposal to build a Configuration Management Method, the following is a checklist of features you would require from it:
- configuration items can be created, amended and deleted
- configuration items are uniquely identified
- the owner of each configuration item is identified
- the owner of a configuration item can be changed without changing the item itself
- baselines can be established
- configuration audits can be performed
- it should be possible to restore the system to its state as at a previous baseline, either temporarily or permanently
- changes from any baseline can be tracked
- the placing of a Configuration Item in the system library is controlled and documented
- Impact Analysis can be carried out to help assess the ramifications of changing one or more configuration items
- Configuration Items which are of interest to more than one project can be held centrally
- in order to aid Impact Analysis the Configuration Management Method should provide a structure which defines the relationships between Configuration Items, so that no Configuration Item is changed without knowing the effect on other products

7 | Controlling Quality

Introduction

Quality is like a carpet's underlay. It improves the product, gives it a longer life, but you can't add it on last as an afterthought. You have to plan for it and add it at the right time.

Quality Definitions

The PRINCE manual quotes the definition of quality from British Standard 4778:

>the totality of features and characteristics of a product
>or service which bear on its ability to satisfy a given need.

In the case of a project the 'given need' is defined by the user's requirements.

Quality Assurance

Quality Assurance sets down the procedures to be followed to inspect quality, obtain agreement with the users on the level of quality sought, validate and monitor the effectiveness of the inspection procedures themselves, and lays down the quality responsibilities. It defines the audit trail which must be available for the user or an outside Quality Assurance group to inspect the amount and level of the quality reviews being done. This includes the testing activities.

Quality Control

Quality Control is the examination of products produced by the project. These products may be technical, management or quality ones. This examination might be done via testing or a quality review. In both cases there should be criteria against which the product can be measured in order to define whether or not it is acceptable.

The task of controlling quality within a project can be divided into:

- agreeing quality criteria for products with the users prior to their production
- planning and resourcing quality reviews and testing
- detecting and correcting quality problems as early as possible
- demonstrating that those quality criteria have been met by the fin-

ished product
- undertaking changes to an existing product in a controlled and documented fashion

The last one of these relates to Controlling Change which is discussed in the next chapter. Quality strategy and planning were discussed in the chapter on the PRINCE Planning Structure. This chapter looks at Product Descriptions and Quality Reviews.

Product Descriptions

The measurement criteria for a product's quality are contained, in PRINCE, within a Product Description. There should be one of these for every product to be created within the project. The creation of the Product Description should be part of the planning process, as the need for a product is identified.

The idea behind Product Descriptions is that the quality requirements for a product should be defined before the product is created. These can then be used as a guide by the person who is to create the product, and as a measure by whoever has the job of checking the quality of the finished product.

The CCTA PRINCE manuals have identified most of the products which will be created in a typical IT project and written Product Descriptions for them. A revised version of each of these appears in Appendix B and can be used for most projects. Each time they should be checked for extra data specific to the project in hand.

A Product Description has the following sections, already explained in Chapter 3:
- Title
- Purpose
- Composition
- Any specific format for the product
- The sources from which the product has been derived
- The quality criteria for the product
- Any priorities in those criteria
- How the conformity of the product with the criteria will be measured

The quality criteria must be measurable, stating any tolerance allowed in each measurement, if any. Appendix B gives examples of acceptable measurements.

Quality Reviews

A Quality Review is a method whereby a product, group of related products, or part of a product is checked by one or more persons against an agreed set of quality criteria. The criteria may comprise the Product Description, standards and a checklist. The purpose of a Quality Review is to identify errors by means of a planned and documented inspection. Another aim of Quality Reviews is to find any errors in products at the earliest possible time and ensure that these are corrected. In his contribution, 'Software Engineering', to IEEE Transactions on Computers in December 1976, Barry Boehm used a graph to describe the correlation between the cost of correcting a fault and how late in the development cycle the fault was found. A copy of this is shown in Figure 7.1.

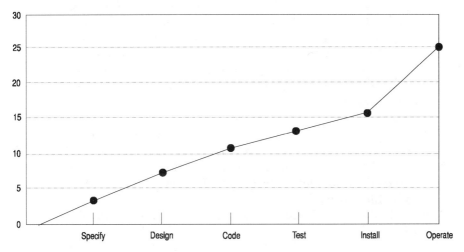

Figure 7.1 Error correction cost – B.Boehm, "Software Engineering" '76

The idea is that the earlier an error is discovered, the less it will have been carried forward into other products and therefore the cheaper it will be to make the correction. Conversely, the later in the development cycle that an error is found, the more expensive it will be to correct it. Back in the 1960's many IT projects left an idea of quality checking until System Test. One reason why this was a major task in those days was that it had to sort out omissions, ambiguities and errors in the user specification and system design as well as any errors met while linking the various programs.

A Quality Review consists of three phases:

Preparation

This covers the administration; identifying the attendees, booking a room, sending out an invitation, plus a copy of the product to be reviewed, its Product Description and any relevant checklists. It also covers the time required by the reviewers to study the product and make a list of the errors which they believe they have found in the product. Any typographical or other obvious small errors are annotated on the product copy. Ideally the error lists should be returned to the chairman of the review before the review to enable an agenda to be made out.

Review

The review is the meeting between reviewers and the presenter, controlled by a chairman, to discuss the list of possible errors and make decisions on any corrective actions needed. The actions are listed and at the close of the review they are allocated to one or more individuals and a target date set for the actions. One or more reviewers are delegated to check that the corrections are done properly.

Follow up

The last phase covers the correction of any action items, confirmation that these are good and have not created errors elsewhere. The action list is signed off and becomes the final part of the Quality Review documentation to be filed away.

The Quality Review roles which must be allocated are those of:

Chairman

The chairman ensures that the review process is properly organised in all three of its steps. In particular this role has the responsibility for the setting of the agenda and the smooth, effective running of the review. The CCTA manuals also suggest that this role should write down any agreed action items.

Presenter

The presenter is the author of the product to be reviewed, unless some unusual event prevents this. One aim of the role is to ensure that the reviewers have everything they need to adequately prepare for the review. This may include a brief presentation during the preparation period. Once in the review, the aim is to answer any questions which the reviewers have.

Reviewer(s)

Reviewers have the job of inspecting the product, asking questions during the review, in order to find any errors in the product. During the Follow-Up phase, one or more reviewers must also confirm that any remedial work has corrected the errors found and not caused harmful side-effects.

Where there is a large group of people attending a review, it is often helpful to the chairman to appoint a scribe to write down the action points. Often the Business Assurance Co-ordinator or Configuration Librarian can fill this role.

An important part of project communication and confidence is to involve the user in Quality Reviews. The user is represented by the User Assurance Co-ordinator and this is often sufficient. But it is important to ensure that the interested parties attend reviews of critical products, rather than merely being represented.

Quality Review Activities
Appendix D contains a list of Quality Review activities for each of the roles involved.

Formal Quality Reviews
A Formal Quality Review is the procedure to be followed in PRINCE when inspecting the major products of the project, where there will be a group of reviewers representing the user and other interested parties. The interested parties will vary according to the product, but will come from such groups as operations, users interfacing systems, the subsequent maintenance group and independent Quality Assurance groups.

One task for the project manager during the planning of a stage is to discuss with the Project Assurance Team which products should be the subject of formal Quality Reviews, and which they wish to attend. An important part of maintaining user confidence and involvement is to ensure that the User Assurance Co-ordinator(s) can select which Quality Reviews they wish to attend. The Stage Quality Plan should identify those products which will be the subject of formal Quality Reviews. Where possible, the chairman of each of these reviews should be identified. In an ideal world all attendees would also be identified in the Quality Plan.

Informal Quality Reviews
Not all products will warrant a group being gathered to inspect them, and there isn't enough time to do this anyway. For a lot of the smaller products an informal Quality Review will be sufficient. An informal Quality Review will usually be one person checking the work of another.

Although described as 'informal', the same Quality Review phases, steps and documentation must be observed. The roles will be shared between attendees. The person reviewing the product would also take the chairman's role.

Even informal Quality Reviews must provide the Business Assurance Co-ordinator with a copy of each piece of Quality Review documentation, as these form part of the evidence of quality checking being performed.

In summary, every product in a PRINCE project must be Quality Reviewed, either formally or informally.

Possible Quality Review Results
A Quality Review can be declared complete or incomplete by the chairman. If a review runs its natural course it is complete. An incomplete one will have been terminated for one reason or another.
Reasons for Declaring a Quality Review Incomplete
- insufficient reviewers turn up for the review
- 'key' reviewers are missing
- the relationships between the attendees is such that the chairman feels inadequate progress is likely to be made
- the product has so many errors it becomes pointless to continue

Exception Memos
Exception Memos record deviations from the planned Quality Review dates. They should be raised by the Chairman of the relevant Quality Review or the Stage Manager and sent to the Business Assurance Co-ordinator, who will update the plan to show the change. They can be raised by the Business Assurance Co-ordinator if he or she is first to spot a slippage.
The deviation will come to light at one of the following moments:
- when the appointed Chairman of the Quality Review hears from the author that the product will not be ready for review on the planned date
- when the reviewers and presenter cannot be brought together to review the product on the planned date
- when the Stage Manager decides after a review that the product should be reworked and a new review scheduled
- when the Stage Manager decides that a halted review should be rescheduled with different reviewers
- when the Stage Manager decides that an incomplete review should be abandoned without correcting the errors found
- when the Stage Manager decides that an unfinished review should be declared complete.

Figure 7.2 shows these possibilities graphically.
It is the job of the Business Assurance Co-ordinator to update the Technical Plan, provide the Stage Manager with a copy of the memo and updated plan, and file the Exception Memo in the Quality File.

Summary
It is often a strange experience, talking to project managers about quality. At the beginning when you talk about 'building a quality product' they nod

their heads and agree this is one of their aims. But when you get down to the detail of writing Product Descriptions before developing the products, Quality Reviews – the documentation and resource needs, keeping a Quality file, they begin to back off, saying 'This seems a lot of overhead.'

The work to ensure quality is not an overhead, any more than putting paint on a car, or a major function in a computer system. You are meeting a user requirement.

You can't guarantee quality by using top university graduates or purchasing expensive development tools. You have to organise for quality, you have to perform activities which are specifically checking for quality (or the lack of it). It needs Project Board support (insistence!). It needs the support of the user. It needs the support of the company senior management. Even with this support it will not happen automatically. It is an integral activity in the production of every product. That is why the Configuration Librarian should not accept any product into the library which has not passed a Quality Review.

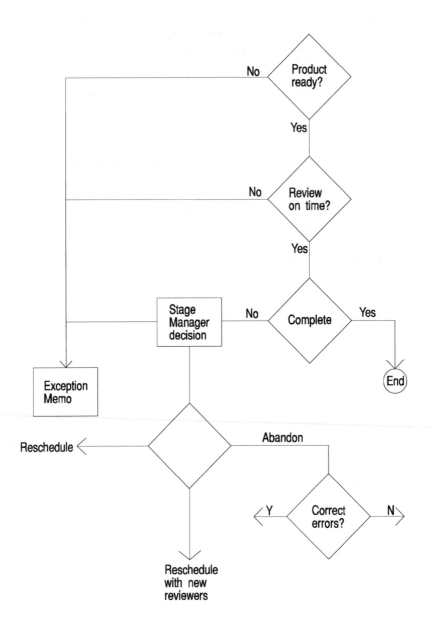

Figure 7.2 Quality review deviations

8 | Controlling Change

No matter how well planned a project has been, if there is no control over changes, this will destroy any chance of bringing the project in on schedule and to budget. In any project there will be changes for many reasons:

- government legislation has changed and this must be reflected in the system specification
- the user changes mind on what is wanted
- because the development cycle is making the user think more and more about the system, extra features suggest themselves for inclusion
- there is a merge of departments, change of responsibilities, company merger or take-over which radically alters the Terms of Reference
- the developer finds that it will be impossible to deliver everything within the agreed schedule or cost
- the developer cannot meet an acceptance criterion, such as performance
- a product delivered by an outside contractor or another system fails to meet its specification

All of these need a process to control them and their effect on the project. This process must make sure they are not ignored, but that nothing is implemented of which the appropriate level of management is unaware. This includes the Project Board. In PRINCE all possible changes are handled by a set of procedures under the heading of Technical Exceptions.

Apart from controlling possible changes, it provides a formal entry point through which all points can be raised. It is the connecting link between Quality Reviews and the rest of the project:

- where an error is found during Quality Review which belongs to a different product than the one under review
- where work to correct an error found during Quality Review cannot be done during the agreed Follow Up period.

Technical Exceptions

There are three types of Technical Exception document in PRINCE:

- Project Issue Reports
- Requests For Change
- Off-Specification

They are used to record desired change to, or some failure in the project's products. It is part of the Configuration Librarian's role to control Technical Exceptions.

Project Issue Report

A Project Issue Report is the formal way into a project of any enquiry, complaint or request outside the scope of a Quality Review Question List. It can be raised by anyone associated with the project about anything, for example:

- a desired new or changed function
- a failure of the project in meeting some aspect of the user requirements. In such cases the report should be accompanied by evidence of the failure and, where appropriate, sufficient material to allow someone to recreate the failure.
- a question about a possible misunderstanding
- a problem with a plan
- a failure of communication

In other words, there is no limit to the content of a Project Issue Report beyond the fact that it should be about the project.

Anything raised at a Quality Review normally goes on an Action List. The exception is if an error is detected in a product which is not the one being reviewed. Such errors are put onto a Project Issue Report as the way of getting them into the system.

When considering the procedures for handling Project Issues, there is the possibility that the subject will be outside the scope of the project. An example might be a bug in a compiler. Although it is being used in the project it clearly has a wider implication. There should be a procedure to close the issue off as far as the project is concerned and transfer it to a departmental level.

The Configuration Librarian will log receipt of the Project Issue Report, allocate the unique identifier, and pass a copy back to the originator and to each member of the Project Assurance Team. The Project Issue Report is now classed as open.

All unresolved Project Issue Reports are reviewed at regular meetings, called and chaired by either the Stage Manager or the Business Assurance Co-ordinator and attended by the Project Assurance Team. The issues are evaluated with the aim of making recommendations to the Project Manager on their resolution. The outcome is normally one of the following:

- The issue has been raised due to a misunderstanding by the originator. The misunderstanding should be explained to the originator and the issue closed.
- The issue is proposing a change to a baselined Configuration Item. A Request For Change should be raised and the issue closed.

- The issue requests a change to the agreed user specification, acceptance criteria or a Product Description. A Request For Change should be raised and the issue closed.
- A product does not meet its specification. An Off-Specification should be raised and the issue closed.
- More evaluation is required
- The issue was received too recently for any evaluation.

The frequency of such meetings will depend on the volume of issues being received, but it should be held regularly and with sufficient frequency to ensure that no inordinate delay occurs in taking action.

The Project Issue Reports and recommendations are submitted to the Project Manager who decides on the action to take.

The Project Issue Reports and the recommendations of the Project Assurance Team will normally be batched and studied by the Project Manager on a frequent and regular basis. The Project Manager has the option of doing this alone or in a meeting with the Project Assurance Team, which has the advantage of further explanation and the team's opinions on the impact on schedule, cost and any other ramifications.

All Project Issue Reports have to be closed by the end of the project. As can be seen from the flow diagram in Figure 8.1, it can only be closed in the ways mentioned in the recommendations above.

Request For Change

A Request For Change is the document on which is recorded a proposed modification to the user requirements. It can only be raised on the authority of the Project Manager as a result of assessment of a Project Issue Report.

Where Requests For Change have been authorised, the relevant Project Issue Reports are returned to the Configuration Librarian. An entry is made on the log for Requests For Change, a Request For Change form is written out and given the unique identifier indicated on the log. The originating Project Issue Report is logged as closed with the appropriate Request For Change identifier and date added to its log and form. The original Project Issue Report is then filed and a copy sent to its originating author.

The new Request For Change now requires analysis to see how much work is involved. This is normally done by the Technical Assurance Co-ordinator, who may request additional help. Part of this work is called Impact Analysis, where the Configuration Librarian helps identify what other products or Configuration Items will be affected. It is particularly important that the librarian identifies any baselined Configuration Items which will need to change. This is because the Project Board will have been told of the completion of those items. Any change to such items must be

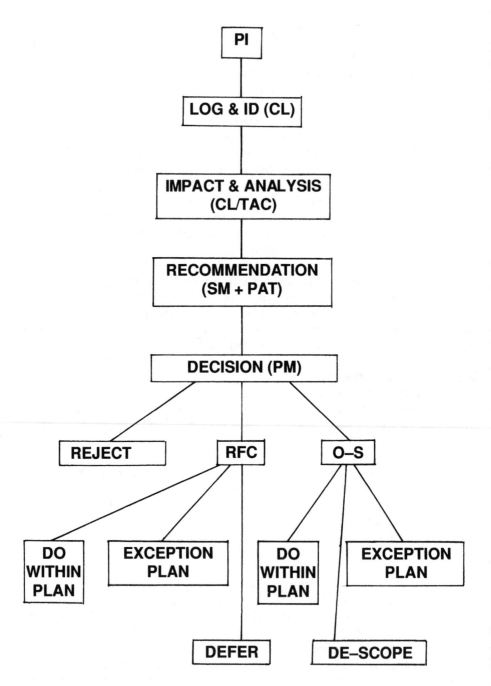

Figure 8.1 Project Issue Flow

approved by the Project Board.

The Business Assurance Co-ordinator costs the identified work and assesses the impact on the stage plan's budget and schedule. For the next decision the Project Manager will want to know if any of the work could be done within the tolerance levels of the current plan. For this reason it is best that a batch of requests are studied, to give a wider view of the effect on the plans.

In preparation for the next decision, the Requests For Change have to be awarded a priority rating. This can be one of four:

- high
- medium
- low
- cosmetic

The PRINCE manuals suggest that the Technical Assurance Co-ordinator determines the priority. It seems more correct that the user's opinion on priority is sought. Therefore it should be the job of the User Assurance Co-ordinator to canvas the users and provide the priority rating.

In order for the Request For Change to be implemented, it must be approved by either the Project Manager or the Project Board. Whose decision it is depends on the following:

- If it is not a change to a Configuration Item which has already been baselined *and* the work can be done within the current plan's tolerances, the Project Manager *can* make the decision to implement it. Alternatively it can be passed to the Project Board for its decision. Since experience shows that there will be a lot of changes during the project, it is a good idea to make the Project Board decide on any changes other than trivialities. This keeps the board aware of how many changes are being requested and their cumulative impact on the schedule and cost. If the stage plan runs into trouble later, it is usually too late for the Project Manager to get any sympathy about a claim that lots of requests have been actioned without asking for more time or money. The answer will usually be 'Why didn't you ask us? We could have cancelled or delayed some of them.'
- If the change is to one or more Configuration Items which the Project Board have already been told are complete (to any baseline, not necessarily the final one), the decision must be made by the Project Board. More than anything, this is to retain the confidence level of the board. If it has been told that something is finished and later find out that it has been changed without consultation, its sense of being in control evaporates.
- If the work to do the Request For Change cannot be done within the tolerance levels of the current Stage Plan, the decision on action must come from the Project Board. The Project Manager must submit an

Exception Plan with the Request For Change, showing the new schedule and cost for the rest of the stage.

- The Senior User on the Project Board is the key role in its decisions on whether to implement the changes. The Configuration Librarian therefore passes to the Senior User all those Requests For Change which have not been decided by the Project Manager. It is the Senior User's job to put them in order of priority for consideration by the board.
- The Project Board's decision may be to:

    implement the change. If the change required an Exception Plan, then this means approving the Exception Plan.

    delay the change to an enhancement project after the current one is finished

    defer a decision until a later meeting

    ask for more information

    cancel the request.

The decision should be documented on the request and the Request For Change log, and an updated copy filed in the Quality File. Whenever its status changes, a copy should be sent to the originator.

The Stage Manager is responsible for scheduling any approved changes. This work will possibly involve the issue of a copy of one or more products by the Configuration Librarian.

On receipt of a completed Request For Change the Configuration Librarian should ensure that any amended products have been re-submitted to the configuration library. The Quality File should be updated with the finalised request, the log annotated and the originator advised.

Off-Specification Report

An Off-Specification Report is used to document any situation where the system fails to meet its specification in some respect. It can only be raised with the authority of the Project Manager after study of a Project Issue Report.

The Configuration Librarian allocates the next unique Off-Specification Report identifier from the log, annotates and closes the originating Project Issue Report, sends a copy of the issue to its author and files the updated issue in the Quality File.

The Technical Assurance Co-ordinator with the help of the Configuration Librarian carries out an Impact Analysis to discover which products are affected by the Off-Specification Report, and then assesses the effort needed.

If it is discovered that the Off-Specification has been raised in error, and should have been a Request For Change, the Off-Specification Report is closed and the original Project Issue Request revived, suitably commented.

Both logs are updated and the originator informed.

As with Requests For Change, the decision on action is taken by either the Project Manager or Project Board:

- If the Off-Specification does not involve a change to a Configuration Item which has already been baselined *and* the work can be done within the current plan's tolerances, the Project Manager *can* make the decision to implement it.
- If the Off-Specification requires changes to one or more Configuration Items which the Project Board have already been told are complete (to any baseline, not necessarily the final one), the decision must be made by the Project Board.
- If the work to do the Off-Specification cannot be done within the tolerance levels of the current Stage Plan, the decision on action must come from the Project Board. The Project Manager must submit an Exception Plan with the Off-Specification Report, showing the new schedule and cost for the rest of the stage.
- The Project Board's decision may be to:
  correct the fault. If the work required an Exception Plan, then this means approving the Exception Plan.
  delay correction of the fault to an enhancement project after the current one is finished
  defer a decision until a later meeting
  ask for more information

The decision should be documented on the Off-Specification Report and its log, and an updated copy filed in the Technical File. Whenever its status changes, a copy should be sent to the originator.

The Stage Manager is responsible for scheduling any approved work to correct Off-Specifications. This work will possibly involve the issue of a copy of one or more products by the Configuration Librarian.

On receipt of a corrected Off-Specification Report the Configuration Librarian should ensure that any amended products have been re-submitted to the configuration library. The Technical File should be updated with the finalised Off-Specification Report, the log annotated and the originator advised.

The Quality File

There is one Quality File for each PRINCE project. It is created by and remains the responsibility of the Business Assurance Co-ordinator. If a Configuration Librarian has been appointed to the project it is important that the duties with regard to the Quality File are clearly defined between this role and the Business Assurance Co-ordinator. Normally the Configuration Librarian will be allocated the duties of logging and filing all the documents.

The Quality File contains the forms which are produced as part of the quality controls applied during the life of the project. If you recall what was said under the heading of 'Quality Assurance' at the beginning of this chapter, it is an important part of the audit trail which can be followed by the user or an independent Quality Assurance body to assess what quality checking has been carried out and how effective it has been. As such, it is a deliverable product.

Wherever possible the originals of documents should be filed in the Quality File. A copy can be filed if the original has to be circulated for signature or comments, but on its return the original should be replaced in the Quality File.

The Quality File should have sections for:

Quality Review Log

Each quality review should have a uniques number to connect the various forms and provide the basis for statistics on how many reviews have been carried out.

Quality Review Invitations

On filing this document the Business Assurance Co-ordinator should check that there is no unreported date slippage compared to the planned review date. If there is, an Exception Memo is raised, the Technical Plan amended and the Stage Manager notified.

Quality Review Result Notifications

If the review was terminated prematurely, the other review documents such as Follow Up Action List, annotated product copies, Question Lists may be attached. These should all be passed to the Stage Manager, a copy of the Result Notification being filed in the Quality File. The original Result Notification form should be returned updated with the Stage Manager's decision plus either an Exception Memo or an Off-Specification Report. The updated review form replaces the copy in the Quality File, the Exception Memo or Off-Specification Report are dealt with by their normal procedures.

Quality Review Follow Up Action Lists

When all corrective actions on the list have been taken and the list signed off by the Chairman of the review, it is filed here.

Technical Exception and Exception Memo Log

All Exception Memos, Project Issue Reports, Off-Specifications and Requests For Change need a unique number. There may be a log for each type of document or a separate one for the three types of Technical Excep-

tion. Standards for the numbering should be included
in the Configuration Management Plan.
Exception Memos
Project Issue Reports
Request For Change
Off-Specifications are regarded as technical documents and filed with the
technical product.

9 | Stage Assessments

Receiving reports on a regular basis allows the user and management to monitor project progress, but is inadequate to give a feeling of complete control. There should be moments in a project when the user and management can formally ask questions of the project manager and compare those views with those of independent observers.

One reason for breaking a project into stages is to provide the user with a number of points in a project at which the progress so far can be reviewed before committing resources to the next stage.

The previous chapters have discussed how PRINCE controls events on a day-to-day basis, mainly on a technical level. This chapter looks at those management controls which occur at selected moments during the project. The controls are *End-Stage Assessments* and *Mid-Stage Assessments*. Both are face-to-face meetings between Project Manager and Project Board, where the Project Manager needs formal written approval to carry on with the project.

This links back to the subject of dividing a project into stages for the purpose of such meetings, discussed in Chapter 4, Planning a Project.

End-Stage Assessment

Objectives
This is a mandatory management control point at the end of each stage. The assessment gives approval for the work to date and provides authority to proceed to the next stage. A stage cannot be considered complete until it has received this formal approval.

The aim is for the Project Board to assure themselves that:
- the products of the current stage have all been delivered
- the products have been reviewed and are of good quality
- the products meet the user requirements at this point
- the stage was completed within budget and schedule tolerances
- the project is still within the tolerances laid down by the IT Executive Committee
- a viable business case still exists for the project
- the next stage has been planned and is acceptable to them in terms of its deliverables, quality plan, schedule and budget

Participants
- Project Board
- Project Manager
- Project Assurance Team (with the exception of the Configuration Librarian)
- Current Stage Manager
- Next Stage Manager

Preparation
1. There should be no surprises at the meeting. The Project Manager and User Assurance Co-ordinator should have been in regular contact with the Senior User role to ensure that there is no major problem with any of the products. The Technical Exception controls should have been used if there was a problem. The stage should still be within its tolerances. Otherwise an Exception Plan should have been raised at the time the knowledge of the deviation came to light.
2. If the Project Manager foresees any difficulties with the next stage when preparing the plans, there should be a discussion with the Project Board before the End-Stage Assessment.
3. The Configuration Librarian should provide to the Project Manager a Configuration Status Account, confirming that all expected products and baselines have been achieved.
4. The Business Assurance Co-ordinator has to update the Stage and Project Resource Plans with the actuals.
5. The Project Manager has a review made of the project Business Case. This is normally done by the Business Assurance Co-ordinator and the User Assurance Co-ordinator.
6. The Project Manager and current Stage Manager prepare a brief report on the stage.
7. The Project Manager and next Stage Manager prepare the next Stage Plans with the help of the Project Assurance Team. The Project Manager may wish to approach the Project Board with a suggestion for the tolerance level to be allowed, if it is felt that this should for any reason be different to the tolerance percentage passed down by the IT Executive Committee.
8. The User Assurance Co-ordinator should confirm that the level of quality reviews planned for the next stage are adequate.
9. The Project Manager, Business Assurance Co-ordinator and User Assurance Co-ordinator review the project Business Case in the light of the next Stage Plans.
10. The Configuration Librarian should provide the Project Manager with statistics on the Technical Exceptions; numbers actioned, outstanding and cancelled.

11. The documents for the End-Stage Assessment should be circulated before the meeting in time for the attendees to read them.

Timing

In theory the timing should be as follows. The current stage should finish, actuals be gathered in, the next stage be planned. Then the End-Stage Assessment should be held. If the project is approved to continue, the next stage can then begin. In practice the question would be 'What do we do with the team between the end of one stage and the start of the next?' Work doesn't normally stop, although it can. Such a situation is most likely to arise where there really is doubt about the continuation of the project.

Normally the End-Stage Assessment should be held just before the end of a stage. This means that some of the 'actuals' will have to be more of a forecast, and one or two products will not be finished. The amount 'forecast' should be literally only a few days, and the User Assurance Co-ordinator should be in a position to make an interim assessment of any unfinished products. The essential points are that:

- the End-Stage Assessment should occur very close to the end of a stage when a valid appraisal of its results can be made
- very little of the next stage's expenditure should be undertaken, if any, without Project Board approval of its plans

Agenda

1. The Project Manager presents a brief report on the results of the current stage. This should summarise performance under the headings:
   schedule
   budget
   quality
   the impact of technical exceptions
2. The appropriate member of the Project Assurance Team reports on:
   user satisfaction with the products and communication
   the quality checking work carried out and its results
   the adherence to the use of the standards
   the status of Technical Exceptions
3. The Project Manager reviews the outstanding Off-Specifications, their impact on system functions and acceptance criteria.
4. The Project Manager gives a project re-assessment in the light of the stage results.
5. The Business Assurance Co-ordinator reviews the project Business Case in the light of results so far.
6. The Project Manager and next Stage Manager present the next Stage Plans, including the approach, assumptions and risks.

7. The Project Manager reviews any impact the next Stage Plans would have on the Project Plans and the project Business Case.
8. The Project Assurance Team present their assessments of the next Stage Plans.
9. The Project Board make the decision whether to approve the next Stage Plans or not. The End-Stage Approval form is signed by each member of the Project Board and dated. If the decision is to stop the project, the Executive notes the reasons on the End-Stage Approval form. It is then the Executive's job to advise the IT Executive Committee.

Mid-Stage Assessment

A Mid-Stage Assessment is a similar formal meeting to the End-Stage Assessment between the same attendees. The major purpose is again to obtain the Project Board's approval to continue. There are four different situations which can lead to the need for a Mid-Stage Assessment:

- if the stage is a long one, say three months or more. In such a long stage the Project Board should want to satisfy itself that the stage is progressing satisfactorily, and ensure that any problems are being dealt with correctly. This keeps up the board's confidence in the project and refreshes the communication lines.
- when stage tolerance levels have been exceeded, or the Project Manager is advised that they will be exceeded in the near future. The presentation to the Project Board examines the cause of the deviation, the possible actions and recommends one of these. An Exception Plan must be put forward in line with the recommendation. It has to cover the period from the present moment to the end of the stage.
- when a Request For Change or Off-Specification is needed to be actioned and cannot be done within the tolerances of the current plan. Again an Exception Plan has to be put forward at the Mid-Stage Assessment to cover the work, covering the rest of the stage.
- when the Project Manager feels that it would be advantageous to begin work on part of the next stage before the End-Stage Assessment can be held for the present stage. The plan should be for the amount of work to be done before the End-Stage Assessment of the present stage is held.

The attendees are the same as for the End-Stage Assessment and the agenda is similar. There is no full next Stage Plan to be presented. For the first situation it is the current Stage Plans, for the next three an Exception Plan, and for the last situation, a small part of the next Stage Plan.

10 | Controlling Deviations from Plan

Tolerance

In Chapter 3 when discussing plans we mentioned tolerance. This chapter starts with a review of why tolerances are needed.

No plan ever created has been met 100%. It is not humanly possible to plan a series of activities for several resources over a length of time such as we are talking about for a PRINCE project or stage, and meet that plan exactly every step of the way, every day of the plan. Some things will get done a little earlier than expected, others a little later. There may be tasks we have forgotten, others which prove not to be needed. There are a hundred and one things about the future which we cannot guarantee; sickness, resource performance, the response of resources outside our control, and so on. It is for reasons such as these that tolerances are needed.

Deviations

When the Project Board gives the Project Manager approval to do some work, that approval is on the basis of a plan submitted to them. The idea of Project Board control in PRINCE is that the Project Manager only has approval to continue if he or she sticks to that plan. Any deviation and it's back to the Project Board to explain what has gone wrong and present a new plan. So if you spend one pound more than planned the first week, is that a sufficient deviation to warrant recalling the Project Board? If in a three month plan a product gets completed on Tuesday instead of Monday, is that a deviation? The answer is yes, it is a deviation. But a very small one. The kind that is likely to happen each week. The Project Board would get very annoyed if it was recalled for trivial deviations like that.

So where do we draw the line between what is a significant deviation and what is not? It is hardly in line with what we have said about control to allow Project Managers to use their judgment. That is why tolerance levels are set. The Project Manager tries to meet the plan exactly, but as long as any deviations stay within the tolerance levels set by the Project Board, they are not significant.

Project and Stage Tolerance Levels

Figure 10.1 reminds you of the Resource Graph which we drew up in Chapter 3. It shows the tolerance margins on either side of the plotted cost line. We have added a line showing the actual costs being plotted over the first two stages. We can see that there have been deviations, but these have stayed within the tolerance margins.

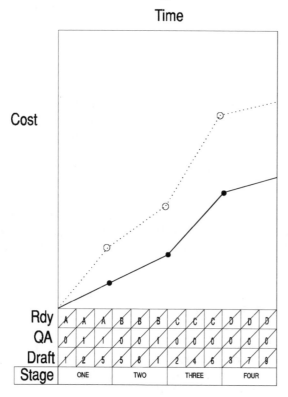

Figure 10.1 Updated Project Resource Graph

The IT Executive Committee should pass down to the Project Board as part of their Terms of Reference a rough idea of how much they expect the project to cost, how long they expect it to last and a tolerance level, usually expressed as a percentage. This idea will have come from an earlier investigation such as a Feasibility Study. If this information is not available, then the Project Board have to think of a reasonable project tolerance when discussing the Project Plan with the Project Manager. Having gone through the planning process, the Project Manager will be in a good position to advise how definite or provisional the future looks.

The project tolerance levels give a guide to the stage tolerance levels. There is not much point in setting a ten per cent tolerance for the project and then allowing a twenty per cent tolerance on one stage. Stages tend to vary within the project tolerance, using it as a maximum, and often being able to decrease in the later stages by when there are fewer unknowns.

If at any Stage Assessment it looks as though the project cannot be completed within its tolerance levels, the Project Board, through the Executive, has to go back to the IT Executive Committee and obtain a decision from then.

Exception Plans

If it appears that a stage cannot be completed within its tolerances, the Project Manager must advise the Project Board immediately and call for a Stage Assessment meeting. At that meeting an Exception Plan must be presented. The reasons for such a meeting are:

- the stage tolerance set by the Project Board has been, or will soon be exceeded. This might be the budget tolerance, schedule tolerance or both.
- one or more Requests For Change have been agreed by the Project Board which cannot be done within the present Stage Plan tolerances
- it is necessary to correct an Off-Specification situation within the stage, but this cannot be done within the stage tolerances

An Exception Plan consists of three things:

- a Technical Plan covering the activities needed from the present moment to the end of the Stage
- a matching Resource Plan
- additional information to describe the exception, the options examined and the recommended course of action. This course of action is the one shown in the Technical and Resource Plans

The additional information should include:

- a description of the exception situation
- an explanation of the circumstances which led to that situation
- a prediction of the impact of the exception on cost, schedule, quality or other element of the Stage and Project if no action is taken
- the options considered
- any assumptions being made in these options
- the recommendation, together with reasons for it and why the other options were discounted
- the impact of the recommended plan on the Stage, Project Plan and Business Case

Mid Stage Assessments

The Exception Plan is presented formally to the Project Board at a Mid-Stage Assessment. 'Presented formally' means that the board should already have been informed and sounded out in general terms about the options.

Chapter 9 discussed the general format of a Mid-Stage Assessment, so that will not be repeated here. If the Project Board agree to the Exception Plan, it becomes the Stage Plan. This reinforces the point that an Exception Plan contains all the work still to be done in the Stage, not just the extra or modified activities.

The Project Board may well insist on more frequent reports for the period of the Exception Plan to ensure that they are kept fully informed, particularly if they feel that the exceptional circumstance should have been avoided by the Project Manager.

11 | Project Closure

In the past it often proved difficult to bring a project to a formal close. Many seemed to drift on and on. There were usually a number of reasons for this:

- At the beginning of the project it was not agreed what would be the measurements for the successful completion of a project. Thus at what the developer thought was the end of what was committed to be done, the user complained that more (or better) was expected. In PRINCE during the production of the Project Initiation Document we discussed the establishment of Acceptance Criteria for just this purpose. If the end-product meets all criteria, there can be no objection to closure of the project.
- The second reason was failure to formally agree on the specification of the product before developing a solution. At the end, everyone had a different idea of what was originally requested. PRINCE puts responsibility for approving the specification in the job description of the Senior User. It would also be the subject of a Quality Review and one of the major products to be assessed at an End Stage Assessment.
- A third reason was the failure to control changes to specification during the project. By the time the expected end of the project arrived it was unclear to all what the end-product should look like. In fact, changes were still rolling in, the end-product was a moving target, there was never any agreement on what the end-product should look like and it was impossible to end the project on a satisfactory note. Under the PRINCE methodology all changes are strictly documented and controlled, linking to Project Board agreement and, where necessary, to Exception Plans for their implementation.
- The fourth reason was the lack of a formal procedure to close a project. PRINCE provides such a procedure and identifies appropriate sign-off documents, their timing and whose signatures are needed.

Project Evaluation Review

Under PRINCE guidelines, one of the documents submitted to the Project Closure meeting is a Project Evaluation Review. This is written by the Project Manager with the help of the Project Assurance Team, and can be started at any time during the installation step. It reviews the performance of the project. Its purpose is to document any lessons which can be learned for the benefit of future projects.

The minimum headings under which the review is written are:

Performance

An assessment of the project's achievement of the objectives defined in the Project Initiation Document. Also a comparison of planned and actual duration, cost and resource usage. To provide the full picture, this should include statistics about the extra effort caused by approved Requests For Change, and of the estimated effort it would have taken to correct Off-Specifications which were not implemented.

Productivity

comment on the effectiveness of any development techniques or products used. This is particularly useful if they can be compared to similar projects which did not use them.

Quality

Full statistics of the Quality Reviews carried out; how many, number of errors found, correction time, any common cause of the errors. Also details of the Technical Exceptions raised by stage; number, type, priority, effort, number implemented, cancelled and held over.

Development Methods

experience of any techniques or other development aids used, including any suggestions for their future use or changes to them.

Project Management

comments on the project management procedures used, highlighting anything found particularly effective, ineffective or bad. The highlights should include the assessed impact of that element and make suggestions for the benefit of future projects.

Acceptance Letters

As the system moves towards completion and installation, there are four, possibly five, Acceptance Letters which have to be signed by Project Board members:

- System Acceptance Letter
- User Acceptance Letter
- Operations Acceptance Letter
- Security Acceptance Letter
- Business Acceptance Letter

The last two of these are signed as part of the Project Closure Meeting and are discussed under that heading later in this chapter.

System Acceptance Letter
This has to be signed by the Senior Technical member of the Project Board as representative of the developing team. It is usually prepared by the Project Manager and confirms on behalf of the developing team(s) that the system has passed all their tests, notably any system test, and is ready for delivery to the user.

User Acceptance Letter
This is again probably prepared by the Project Manager, but has to be signed by the Senior User(s). It confirms that the end-products meet the Acceptance Criteria, that the user has run any necessary acceptance tests on the system and is prepared to accept the system for live running.

Operations Acceptance Letter
Signed by the Operations Manager, if there is one, and the Senior User, this confirms on behalf of the staff who will operate the system that they are prepared to accept and operate the system.

Project Closure Meeting
When the system has been installed and is ready to be handed over to maintenance, this final management control is held by the Project Board. Its objective is to close the project in a controlled fashion and report back to the IT Executive Committee. In order to do this, the meeting has to:
- confirm that all products are complete
- confirm that all Project Issue Reports and Quality Review Action lists have been closed
- confirm that all Requests For Change and Off-Specifications have been either closed or recorded as held-over with the approval of the Project Board
- confirm that all products necessary to operate and maintain the live system are available, referenced and filed
- appraise the Project Manager's Project Evaluation Review
- confirm that the Systems, User and Operations Acceptance Letters have been signed
- set up the next CRAMM review (if required). CRAMM stands for CCTA Security Risk Analysis and Management Methodology. It is a package provided by the CCTA to identify and justify the necessary security precautions for IT systems
- set up a Post-Implementation Review at a date when the system will have settled down and its performance can be fully evaluated

- have the Executive sign the Business Acceptance Letter

In order to achieve these points, let us stress again that it is important that in the Project Initiation Document the Acceptance Criteria make clear what will constitute a successful end to the project.

Attendees

- Project Board
- Project Manager
- Stage Manager of the final stage (if used)
- Project Assurance Team

The Project Closure replaces the final End Stage Assessment. Management representing other interests such as Operations and maintenance should also be invited.

The activities to prepare for the Project Closure meeting are listed in Appendix C.

Post-Implementation Review

It is very often impossible to ascertain immediately a project ends whether or not it has produced any or all of its expected benefits. But it is a job which should be done. After all, the project was probably justified on the basis of the expected benefits, and there should be an assessment of whether they have been realised. This will answer user questions about the value for money obtained from the project and will also provide facts which can be used to temper benefit estimates on future projects.

The Post-Implementation Review is held some time after the system has gone live. The length of time depends on the system. It should be allowed enough time for its performance to be tuned under live running conditions, and for the data to be built up to normal operating sizes. If the system runs through several cycles, e.g. weekly, monthly, quarterly and so on, a judgment is needed on how long to wait before doing the review. It must be sufficiently soon for the project to be remembered by the IT Executive Committee!

It is a business assessment of the system produced by the project and is sent to the IT Executive Committee. The Executive of the Project Board is responsible for its being done. The actual investigation and preparation of the document for the Executive to sign will probably be done by members of the maintenance team and system users. Its contents are:

- file sizes
- file growth
- manpower requirements for running the system
- document turn-round times
- response times
- security
- error rates

- delays
- operations from previous systems now superseded
- outstanding problems
- performance of the system against its forecast savings and benefits
- unplanned benefits
- user reaction to the new system

Production of the Post-Implementation Review is the last act of a PRINCE project. The end-product of the project will go on to be enhanced and maintained, but the original project ends here.

Appendix A Product Breakdown Structures

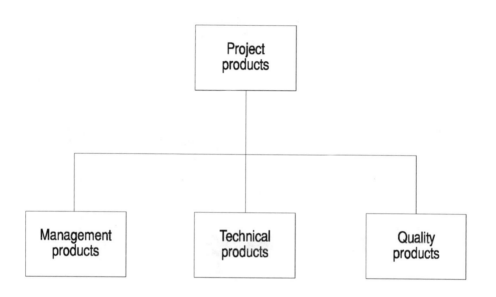

Figure A.1 Product breakdown structure overview

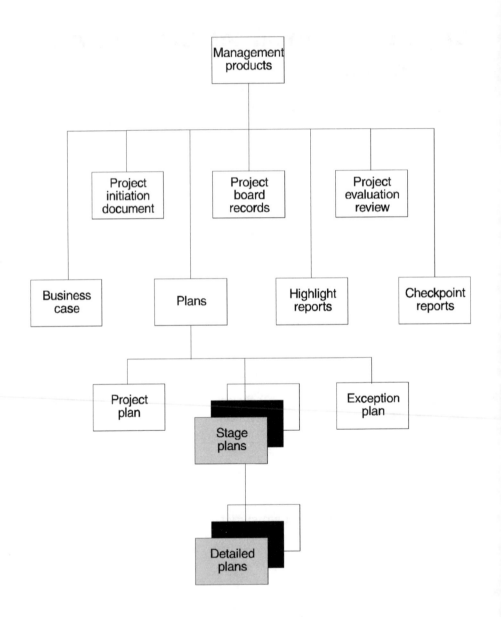

Figure A.2 Management products

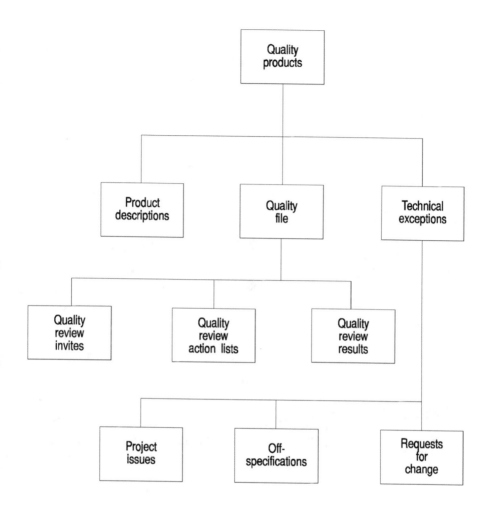

Figure A.3 Quality products

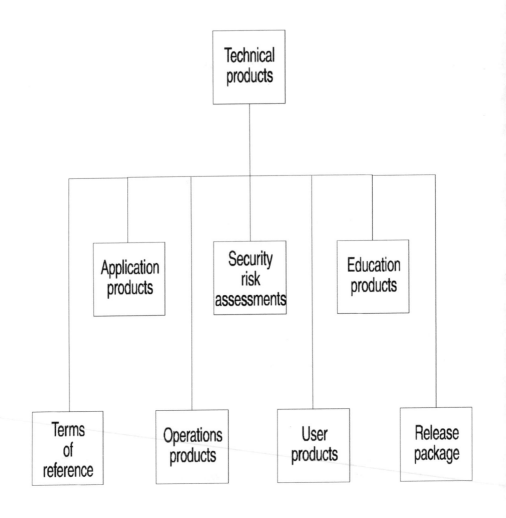

Figure A.4 Technical products

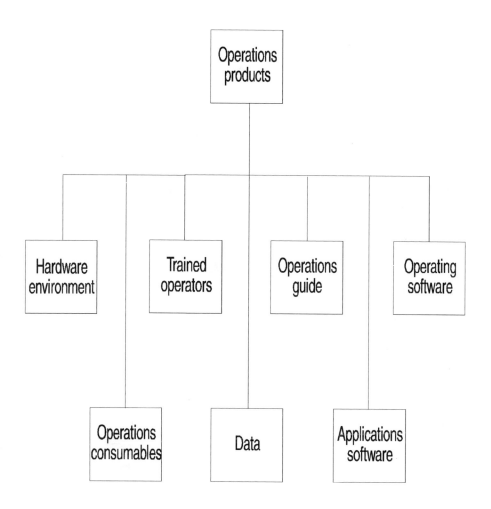

Figure A.5 Operations products

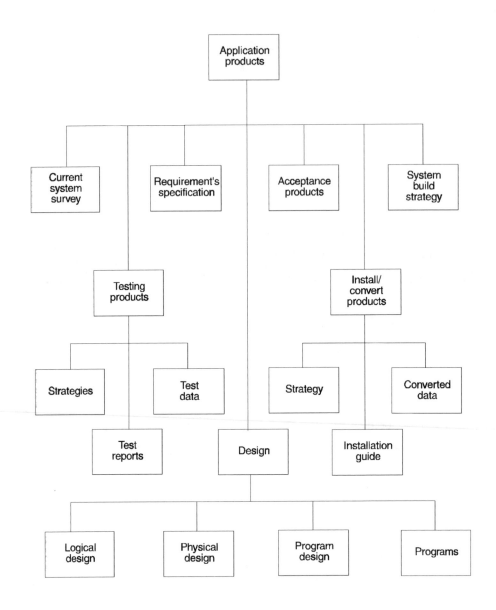

Figure A.6 Application products

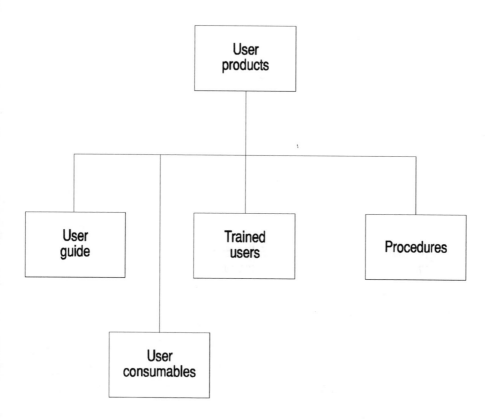

Figure A.7 User products

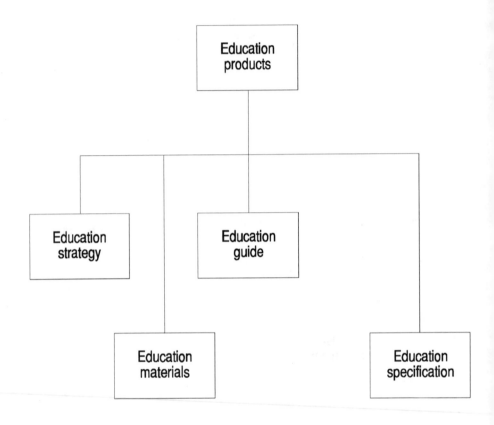

Figure A.8 Education products

Appendix B Product Descriptions

There should be a Product Description for every product to be created in a PRINCE project. Each product should be described under the headings:

- Purpose
- Composition
- Derivation
- Format/Presentation
- Quality Criteria
- Quality Method

The Product Description ensures that the team member to whom the product is allocated has a clear idea of what is required. It also acts as a measurement of the completed product when it is submitted for review.

This appendix contains generic descriptions of the typical products of a computer project. They can be used as templates for any specific project. There are three major sections, following the normal PRINCE breakdown:

- management products
- technical products
- quality products

B1 Management Products

B1.1 Terms Of Reference

Purpose

To document the need for a project, giving the overall purpose and end result sought, the reasons and any management constraints.

Composition

- General statement of need
- Background
- Reasons, including current system limitations
- Objectives of the solution
- Scope and Constraints
- Estimated rate of inflation to be used in any costings
- Acceptance Criteria

Derivation
- Need which cannot be met by current systems
- Project Board

Format/Presentation
- Freeform

Quality criteria
- Contains all the elements listed above
- Approved by the Project Board
- Acceptable to the Project Manager

Quality Method
- Quality Review

B1.2 Project Initiation Document

Purpose
A collection of documents to ensure that the project is begun from a sound business foundation.

Composition
- Terms of reference
- Acceptance criteria
- Organisation chart
- Project plan package
- Project Quality Plan
- Configuration Management Method description
- Next stage plan package
- Stage Quality Plan
- Product descriptions
- Business risk assessment
- Risk proposals
- CRAMM review report (if required)
- Appendices
        Job descriptions
        Plan working documents.

Derivation
- Project Brief
- Feasibility study.

Format/Presentation
- In a binder

Quality Criteria
- All the components are present
- The Project Board have previously discussed and agreed the Terms of Reference
- The plans have been quality reviewed
- The people named have accepted their roles and agreed to the work scheduled in the next stage plan
- All identified high risks have proposals against them.

Quality Method
- Quality Review

B1.3 Business Risk Assessment

Purpose

To identify risks to the project, assess their level of risk and submit proposals to the Project Board for their avoidance or reduction.

Composition
- List of items which might affect the probability of successful completion of the project
- A scale on which the severity of the risk can be assessed
- A weighting of the importance of that risk to the project
- An assessment of the overall risk to the project
- Proposals for avoiding or reducing each severe risk.

Derivation
- Standard checklist
- Project team experience and availability
- Feasibility study.

Format/Presentation
- Standard questionnaire

Quality Criteria
- Each risk assessed or a reason given for its non-applicability
- Overall project risk assessed
- Proposals made for each severe risk (say scoring 15+)
- Where it is thought that no remedial action is possible, this is stated in the proposals.

B 1.4 Project Plan

Purpose
- Identifies all major products of the project
- Specifies the activities needed to produce them
- Schedules their production
- Divides the project into stages and splits the products and activities between stages
- Takes into account constraints of time, resources and budget
- Records project tolerances
- Provides an estimate of the entire project from start to finish
- Specifies the quality strategy and identifies quality control resourcing
- Specifies the Configuration Management Method to be used.

Composition
- Project Technical Plan
- Project Resource Plan
- Project Resource Graph
- Project Quality Plan
- Plan Description.

Derivation
- Terms of Reference
- Feasibility Study Report
- Availability of resources
- Site cost rates
- Site inflation rates for planning purposes.

Format/Presentation
- Technical Plan in bar chart form
- Resource Plan in tabular form showing resources and costs by stage
- Graph of time and cost showing tolerance margins

Quality Criteria
- Meets PRINCE standards
- Correctly reflects the information from which it is derived
- Is acceptable to the Project Board.

Quality Method
- Quality Review

B 1.5 Project Technical Plan

Purpose

A schedule showing the project's major deliverables against a timeframe, any stages into which the project has been divided and major controls such as End-Stage Assessments.

Composition

- Major products to be produced by the project
- Estimated completion dates for each major product
- Number of stages in the project
- Any external dependencies.
- Overall tolerance for the project schedule

Derivation

- Terms of Reference
- Feasibility Study Report

Format/Presentation

Bar chart. The time columns should reflect a period which allows the entire plan to be seen on one page.

Quality criteria

- Meets PRINCE standards
- Correctly reflects the information from which it is derived
- Is acceptable to the Project Board
- Must match the Project Resource Plan.

Quality Method

Quality Review

B 1.6 Project Resource Plan

Purpose

To estimate the amount and cost of each resource type for each stage of the Project Technical Plan.

Composition

- the various stages of the project
- the summary of resources required for each stage
- the cost of these resources.

Derivation
- Terms of Reference
- Availability of resources
- Site cost rates
- Site inflation rates for planning purposes.

Format/Presentation
Tabular form showing resource needs and costs by stage and cumulatively.

Quality criteria
- Meets PRINCE standards
- Correctly reflects the information from which it is derived
- Is acceptable to the Project Board
- Must match the Project Technical Plan.

Quality Method
- Quality Review

B 1.7 Stage Plan

Purpose
- Identifies all the products which the stage must produce
- Specifies the activities needed to produce them
- Defines the resources required by the stage
- Takes into account constraints of time, resources and budget
- Records the stage tolerances
- Provides a fixed reference against which progress of the stage can be measured
- Specifies the quality controls for the stage and identifies the resources needed for them.

Composition
- Stage Technical Plan
- Stage Resource Plan
- Stage Resource Graphical Summary
- Stage Product Breakdown Structure
- Stage Product Flow Diagram
- Stage Activity Plan
- Stage Description.

Derivation
- The Project Plan

- Resource availability.

Format/Presentation
- Technical Plan on a bar chart, tabular form for the Resource Plan, time/cost graph for the Resource Summary

Quality Criteria
- Must be compatible with the Project Plan
- Must be to PRINCE standards
- Must have broken each activity down to ten days or less unless it is to be broken down further in a Detailed Plan
- Must be accepted as reasonable by the Stage Manager.

Quality Method
- Checked against the Project Plans
- Quality Review

B 1.8 Stage Technical Plan

Purpose
To show in detail that portion of the Project Plan to which both Project Manager and Project Board are prepared to commit.

Composition
- All the products and activities of that stage
- A timeframe including target dates for all products
- Resource allocation
- Checkpoints, quality reviews, Mid- and End-Stage Assessments.

Derivation
- The Project Plan
- Stage Activity Network
- Resource availability.

Format/Presentation
- Bar chart. The time unit in the columns should be short enough to see the start and end dates of each activity.

Quality Criteria
- Must be compatible with the Project Plan.
- Must be to PRINCE standards
- Must have broken each activity down to ten days or less unless it is to be broken down further in a Detailed Plan

- Must be accepted as reasonable by the next Stage Manager

Quality Method
- Checked by Technical Assurance Co-ordinator

Quality Review

B 1.9 Stage Resource Plan

Purpose

It is required by the Project Board at the End-Stage Assessment of the previous stage to demonstrate that the project is continuing along the lines of the Project Plan.

Together with the Stage Technical Plan it provides the measurement against actuals to determine the status of the of the stage.

Composition
- Summary of resources required per time period of the Stage Technical Plan
- The cost of the resources
- An accumulative cost of the stage by time period

Derivation
- The Project Plan
- Stage Technical Plan
- Resource costs.

Format/Presentation

Tabular format showing the resource needs by type and costs by week and cumulatively.

Quality Criteria
- Must be compatible with the Project Plan
- Must be compatible with the Stage Technical Plan
- Must be to PRINCE standards
- Must be accepted as reasonable by the next Stage Manager.

Quality Method
- Checked by the Business Assurance Co-ordinator
- Quality Review

B 1.10 Detailed Plan

Purpose

It shows a stage activity in greater detail than the Stage Technical Plan.

Composition
- One activity from the stage plan broken down into sub-activities each lasting only a few days.
- Technical plan
- Resource plan.

Derivation
- Stage Technical Plan
- Resource costs.

Format/Presentation
- Same as Stage Technical Plan

Quality Criteria
- Must be compatible with the Project Plan
- Must be compatible with the Stage Technical Plan
- Must be to PRINCE standards
- Must be accepted as reasonable by the next Stage Manager

Quality Method
- Checked by Technical Assurance Co-ordinator
- Quality Review

B 1.11 Product Breakdown Structure

Purpose

A diagram showing the products to be produced, either as end-products or as interim products required to help produce the end-products. There is a high-level structure for the entire project and a lower-level structure for each stage of the project.

Composition
- Management products
- Technical products
- Quality products

Derivation
- Terms of reference

- PRINCE model (see Chapter 5 Section 4)

Format/Presentation
- Hierarchical structure

Quality Criteria
- Contains the items shown in the standard PRINCE product break-down structure
- Contains any specific end-products mentioned in the terms of reference
- Has an identification method which agrees with site standards
- For a stage product breakdown structure, it can be matched back to the project structure to show its derivation.

Quality Method
- Quality Review

B 1.12 Product Flow Diagram

Purpose
A picture illustrating the sequence of producing the products identified in the Product Breakdown Structure and how they relate to each other. Its aim is to assist in the later creation of an activity network.

Composition
- All the products identified in the associated Product Breakdown Structure plus connecting lines between them to show the sequence of their creation and the inter-dependencies. The sequence should run from top to bottom on the page.
- There is a high-level structure for the entire project and a lower-level structure for each stage of the project.

Derivation
- The relevant (Project or Stage) Product Breakdown Structure
- Model Product Breakdown Structure (Chapter 5 Section 4)
- Model Product Flow Diagram (Chapter 5 Section 5).

Format/Presentation
- Blank or graph paper. Flow is from top of page to bottom. Flow shown by arrowed lines.

Quality Criteria
- Contains the items shown in the standard PRINCE Product Flow

Diagram; at the project level it contains any specific end-products mentioned in the terms of reference
- Has an identification method which agrees with site standards
- For a stage Product Flow Diagram, it can be matched back to the project structure to show its derivation.

Quality Method
- Quality Review

B 1.13 Activity Network

Purpose
A diagrammatic illustration of the activities required by the plan, showing their sequence and any logical constraints between them.

Composition
- Activities to create, change and ensure the quality of all the products identified in the associated Product Flow Diagram, plus connecting arrows between them to show the sequence of their creation and the inter-dependencies. The sequence should run from left to right on the page.
- There is a high-level network for the entire project and a lower-level structure for each stage of the project.

Derivation
- Product Flow Diagram.

Format/Presentation
- See site standards. Flow is from left to right.

Quality Criteria
- Contains activities for all the products in the associated Product Flow Diagram
- Follows site standards for network representation
- Shows activity duration, critical path and floats

Quality Method
- Quality Review

B 1.14 Resource Graph

Purpose
To show in a picture the cumulative cost of the plan. It also lists the

major products to be produced during the planned time and shows the status of them, e.g. whether they have reached draft form, have been Quality Reviewed or have been handed over as complete. When a line showing actual expenditure is added, the additional information on the status of the end-products will add to the understanding of whether the plan is above or below budget.

Composition
- A graph with Time and Cost as the axes
- Time divisions of Stages (for the Project Plan) or a suitable time period (months or weeks) for the Stage Plan
- The major products associated with each time period
- A check box for each product to show its status

Derivation
- Resource Plan.

Format/Presentation
- Graph paper or standard form

Quality Criteria
- Accurately reflects the cumulative costs of the Resource Plan
- Indicates the major products for each period shown.

Quality Method
- Quality Review

B 1.15 Plan Text

Purpose
To put the graphical elements of the plan in context, and complete the information required in order to understand the plan.

Composition
Includes:
- plan description
- quality plan
- plan assumptions
- external dependencies
- plan pre-requisites
- plan risks
- tolerance
- reporting

Derivation
- Terms of reference
- Technical plan
- Site quality standards

Quality Criteria
All composition elements present. Identifies the project/stage level of the plan. Provides all information required by the Project Board to assess the diagramatic plans. Describes all the requirements and assumptions made by the project manager on which the success of the plan relies. It is recommended that the product be quality reviewed by the Project Assurance Team prior to presentation to the Project Board.

B 1.16 Project Quality Plan

Purpose
To define the quality methods which will be used during the project, and to list the major products which will be the subjects of a formal review or test.

Composition
- Statement of understanding of the product quality desired, including the balance between quality, cost and time
- Identification of the Quality Assurance procedures which will be followed
- Identification of the Quality Control method(s) which will be used
- Identification of the Change Control procedures which will be used
- Statement of the major types of test which will be applied to the product at the various stages of its creation
- A list of the major end-products which will be quality reviewed or tested.

Derivation
- Project Product Breakdown Structure
- Product Descriptions.

Format/Presentation
- See Chapter 4

Quality Criteria
- The procedures and method described must exist.
- They must satisfy the user of their completeness and adequacy.

Quality Method
- Quality Review

B 1.17 Stage Quality Plan

Purpose
To list the major products of the stage which will be the subjects of a formal review or test.

Composition
- Statement of the major types of test which will be applied to the products during the stage
- A list of the major end-products which will be quality reviewed during the stage

Derivation
- Stage Product Breakdown Structure
- Product Descriptions

Format/Presentation
- See Chapter 4

Quality Criteria
- The Technical Assurance Co-ordinator must feel that sufficient reviews and tests have been identified to guarantee the quality of the stage products
- Adequate allowance of time and effort for the reviews and tests must have been built into the plan and must be shown separately.

Quality Method
- Quality Review

B 1.18 Exception Plan

Purpose
A re-plan when costs and/or timescales for an approved Stage Plan have, or are about to exceed the tolerance level set for it. It is required in order to get approval from the Project Board to drop the current Stage Plan and proceed on the budget and schedule defined in the Exception Plan.

Composition
- It has the same components as the Stage Plan
- A description of the cause of the deviation from the Stage Plan

- The consequences of the deviation
- The available options
- The Project Manager's recommendations

Derivation
- Current Stage Plans
- Actuals

Format/Presentation
- Same as for Project and Stage Plans

Quality Criteria
- The current Stage Plan must accurately show the status of budget and schedule
- The reason(s) for the deviation must be stated
- The Exception Plan must have both technical and resource plans.

Quality Method
- Quality Review

B 1.19 Highlight Report

Purpose

To provide the Project Board with a brief summary of the stage status at intervals defined by them.

Composition
- Date
- Period covered
- Budget status
- Schedule status
- Products completed during the period
- Actual or potential problems
- Products to be completed during the next period
- Total of Requests For Change approved
- Budget and schedule impact of the changes.

Derivation
- Checkpoint reports
- Technical exception files
- Stage technical plan
- Stage resource plan.

Format/Presentation
Single sheet of paper with three sections; achievements this period, actual or potential problems, achievements next period. Accompanied by a copy of the updated Stage Resource Plan Graphical Summary.

Quality Criteria
- Accurate reflection of checkpoint reports
- Accurate summary of Technical Exception files
- Accurate summary of plan status.

Quality Method
- Checked by Business Assurance Co-ordinator

B 1.20 Checkpoint Report

Purpose
To document at a frequency defined in the stage plan the status of work for each member of the project team.

Composition
- Date held
- Period covered
- Follow-ups from previous reports
- Activities during the period
- Products completed during the period
- Quality work carried out during the period
- Actual or potential problems or deviations from plan
- Work planned for the next period
- Products to be completed during the next period.

Derivation
- Verbal reports from project team members.

Format/Presentation
- Form in three parts; achievements this period, problems or potential problems, achievements next period.

Quality Criteria
- Every item in the stage plan for that period covered
- Every team member working to an agreed schedule
- Every team member's work covered.

Quality Method
- Checked against Checkpoint Reports and Stage Technical Plan

B 1.21 Approval To Proceed

Purpose

Confirmation in writing by the Project Board on the agreed action to be taken at either an End- or Mid-Stage Assessment.

Composition
- Name of the current or next stage
- Names and roles of the Project Board members
- Signatures of each Project Board member
- Comments on any agreed follow-up action or area of concern
- Date of the Approval

Derivation
- End-Stage Assessment meeting.

Format/Presentation
- See form sample in appendix E.

Quality Criteria
- Signature of all Project Board members.

Quality Method
- Quality Review

B 1.22 Project Evaluation Report

Purpose

To provide an assessment of the final product(s) of the project against the Terms of Reference after a period of their operation and document any lessons in the running of the project which will help future projects.

Composition
- A comparison of the project's achievements with the objectives set out in the Project Initiation Document
- Recommendations for future enhancement or modification
- A stage-by-stage summary of actual performance against plan for budget and schedule.
- An description of any abnormal events causing deviations
- An analysis of Technical Exceptions and their results

- An assessment of the project management activity
- Project management recommendations for future projects
- An assessment of technical methods and tools used
- Technical recommendations for future projects
- A Quality Review analysis
- Quality recommendations for future projects.

Derivation
- Project files.

Format/Presentation
- Site standards

Quality Criteria
- Covers all the points above
- Recommendations are sensible and realistic
- Any major failures, flaws or omissions (technical, management or quality) in the product or project are covered.

Quality Method
  Quality Review

B2 Technical Product Descriptions

This part of the appendix offers a description of the typical technical products of a computer project.

B 2.1 Current System Survey

Purpose
  A full description of the current system.

Composition
  Current System Description:
- Data flow diagrams
- User view logical data structures
- List of major functions
- Physical system description
- Hardware usage
- System flowchart
- Interfaces
- Files
- Operational, security and recovery procedures

- Input and output, details of origin/destination, medium, content, volume, frequency, processing, special rules.
- Costs
  maintenance
  user, including data preparation, consumables operations, including back-up and consumables rentals of hardware and software other costs

Problem Definition:
- Current system limitations:
  functionality
  service (e.g. turnaround and volume)
  quality
    number and frequency of errors
    percentage of input errors trapped
    ease of use
  security

Derivation
- Interviews, questionnaires and current system documentation.

Format/Presentation
- Site standards

Quality Criteria
- Is the survey consistent with the Terms of Reference?
- Are the current users prepared to sign the survey as a true record?

Quality Method
- Quality Review

B 2.2 Feasibility Study

Purpose
To review a number of alternative solutions to the problem defined in the Terms of Reference. The solutions are measured against the acceptance criteria and the best one is recommended.

Composition
- Summary of alternatives examined
- Summary of recommendation
- Reasons
- For each possible solution
  general description

system diagram
business summary
risks
measurement against acceptance criteria
data model
interface descriptions
cost/benefit analysis

Derivation
- Terms of reference
- Format/Presentation
- Site standards

Quality Criteria
- Each alternative has been examined realistically
- The cost/benefit analyses were done using realistic figures
- Evaluation of risks was done prior to selection of the recommended solution

Quality Method
- Quality Review

B 2.3 Requirements Specification

Purpose
A detailed description of the needs to be met by the new system, including constraints and known future enhancements.

Composition
User Requirements:
- General description of the system required
- System objectives
- user environment for the new system
- Major functions
- Data flow
- Processes, rules and regulations
- External Interface descriptions
- Security and recovery needs
- Implementation and conversion needs

Constraints:
- Development costs
- User availability during development

- Running costs (user and operations)
- Business schedule
- Future Enhancements

Derivation
- Terms of Reference
- Current system survey
- Feasibility Study document

Format/Presentation
- Site standards

Quality Criteria
- Matches the documents from which it is derived
- Is within the scope and constraints of the Terms of Reference
- Matches the Acceptance Criteria
- The requirements are mutually consistent
- The Senior User(s) are willing to sign it off as a complete and accurate statement of their needs.

Quality Method
- Quality Review

B 2.4 System Build Strategy

Purpose

To specify how the system is to be built, including the sequence of production. It will cross-refer to the Installation and Conversion Strategy.

Composition
- General description
- System build environment
- Differences to the operational environment
- Any test harnesses or simulations required

Derivation
- Requirements specification
- Physical system design
- Installation and Conversion strategy

Format/Presentation
- Site standards

Quality Criteria
- Consistent with the products from which it is derived

Quality Method
- Quality Review

B 2.5 Logical System Design

Purpose

A detailed description in business terms of a design to meet the new requirements. It will not consider how the functions are to be done, which functions are to be automated or manual, nor timings or media.

Composition
- Detailed process descriptions
- Data descriptions
- Data groupings
- Data volumes

Derivation
- Requirements Specification

Format/Presentation
- Site technical standards

Quality Criteria
- Meets all the requirements
- All data elements are described
- There is agreement on each data element description
- Acceptable to the users
- Meets the Acceptance Criteria.

Quality Method
- Quality Review

B 2.6 Physical System Design

Purpose

A system designed to a level with sufficient detail that program specifications can be drawn from it. It will describe how the functions will be carried out, by what method and will include timings.

Composition
- General description
- Required hardware and software environment
- Process descriptions
- Data descriptions
- File descriptions and record layouts
- Interface descriptions
- Organisation
- Security and recovery methods
- Audit processes and data

Derivation
- Logical System Design
- Installation and Conversion Strategy
- System Build Strategy

Format/Presentation
- Site standards

Quality Criteria
- Is based on and consistent with the logical system design
- Meets the needs of the Requirements Specification
- Consistent with the Installation and Conversion Strategy
- Meets the Acceptance Criteria.

Quality Method
- Quality Review

B 2.7 System Test Strategy

Purpose

To define the types of test, methods and responsibilities for system test.
- Composition
- Objectives and standards to be met
- Types of test to be applied
- Source of test data
- Responsibilities
- Control points
- Tools or harnesses required

Derivation
- Acceptance criteria
- Physical system design

- System build strategy

Format/Presentation
- Site standards

Quality Criteria
- Tests the system against the relevant acceptance criteria
- Tests all functions, links and interfaces
- Tests several cycles
- Tests user and operations manuals
- Tests all forms needed by the system
- Tests all error conditions as well as good data
- Approval by the User Assurance Co-ordinator.

B 2.8 Program Specification

Purpose
To enable a programmer to design a program.

Composition
- Purpose
- Process description
- Data flow diagram
- Data model
- Relevant data descriptions
- Special processing rules
- Common modules to be used
- Audit requirements
- Error handling
- Design standards

Derivation
- Physical system design
- Testing requirements

Format/Presentation
- Site standards

Quality Criteria
- Agreement with the physical system design
- Meet site standards.

Quality Method
- Quality Review

B 2.9 Program Design

Purpose

To enable a programmer to code a program.

Composition
- General description
- Data structures
- Program structure
- List of operations
- List of common modules to be used
- Link to any other programs
- Input, output, file and screen formats@bullett = Error message and handling standards
- Test situations and data
- Screen standards
- Coding standards

Derivation
- Program Specification
- Site standards

Format/presentation
- Site standards

Quality Criteria
- Fully meets the specification
- Meets site standards.

Quality Method
- Quality Review

B 2.10 Program

Purpose

To perform the functions described in the process descriptions
- Composition
- Machine-readable source, object and load modules
- Job Control Language/Batch Commands

Derivation
- System Design
- Program Specification
- Program Design

Format/presentation
- Site standards

Quality Criteria
- Performs all the functions specified in the design documents
- Performs correctly and accurately
- Handles error situations and, where possible carries on
- Terminates in a controlled fashion with appropriate error messages when faced with irrecoverable error situations
- The test data has tested each function, selection and loop
- The test data has tested all possible errors
- The code has been annotated to explain the whole program and each module
- Departmental naming and coding standards have been used.

Quality Method
- Quality Review

B 2.11 System Test Report

Purpose

To document system test results and provide assurance for the signature of the System Acceptance Letter.

Composition
- Review of testing activities
- List of outstanding problems
- Summary of resource usage@bullett = Recommendations
- List of tests and their results

Derivation
- System test
- System test strategy

Format/Presentation
- Site standards

Quality Criteria
- Covers all tests made
- Easy to cross-reference against requirements specification
- User Assurance Co-ordinator confirms all tests passed.

Quality Method
- Quality Review

B 2.12 Acceptance Test Strategy

Purpose

To define the tests to be made prior to acceptance by the user and the methods of testing. To prove the system under a simulation of operational conditions.

Composition
- General approach
- Target levels for the thoroughness of testing
- Types of test to be run
- Responsibilities
- Source of test data
- Checkpoints

Derivation
- Project Quality Plan
- Acceptance Criteria

Format/Presentation
- Site standards

Quality Criteria
- Satisfies the technical acceptance criteria
- Consistent with system build strategy
- Consistent with cut-over strategy
- Cost-effective
- Approved by the User Assurance Co-ordinator.

Quality Method
- Quality Review

B 2.13 Acceptance Test Report

Purpose
Description of the acceptance tests carried out and the results.

Composition
- List of types of acceptance tests carried out
- Review of testing activities
- Test data used
- Results
- Summary of resource usage
- List of outstanding problems
- Recommendations

Derivation
- Acceptance criteria
- Acceptance test strategy
- Requirements specification
- User guide
- Operations guide

Format/Presentation
- Site standards

Quality Criteria
- Meets the requirements specification
- Meets the acceptance criteria
- Fits the acceptance test strategy
- Fully tests the system in performance terms
- Checks every part of the user guide
- Checks every part of the operations guide
- Puts the system through sufficient cycles to ensure that no errors are being made in the permanent files
- Tests all error conditions
- Tests the fall-back, back-up and recovery abilities
- Tests the capacity of the system

Quality Method
- Quality Review

B 2.14Installation And Conversion Strategy

Purpose
Definition of the approach to be taken in installing the system in its operational environment.

Composition
- Installation Strategy
  Description
  required hardware and software
  required communications
  installation units (functions which will be installed together)
  installation schedule
- Data Capture and Conversion Strategy
  description of the general strategy, including
  identification of source and medium of all data required by the
  new system, including its current quality
  strategy for the transfer of the data to the new system
  responsibilities
  estimate of resources needed
- Cut-over Strategy
  strategy description
  preservation of current systems
  link to Data Capture and Conversion
  machine time estimates
- Fall-back Strategy
  fall-back circumstances
  fall-back triggers
  fall-back methods
  recovery steps

Derivation
- Requirements Specification

Format/Presentation
- Site standards

Quality Criteria
- The installation plan is feasible
- It makes it clear how all data will be captured
- Cut-over can be achieved with minimum disruption
- Full recovery can be performed up to full user acceptance of the new system.

Quality Method
- Quality Review

B 2.15 Release Package

Purpose
A set of materials on the appropriate media, which provide the software, documentation and procedures required to install and run the system.

Composition
- Bill of materials
- Version identification
- Description of new or changed functions
- List of error reports fixed by this release
- Statement of dates on which support of previous levels will cease
- Pre-requisite hardware
- Pre-requisite operating system and any supporting software
- Programs
- Libraries of subroutines, drivers, utilities (e.g. conversion)
- Job control language
- Installation guide
- Training materials
- User and operations manuals or updates to them
- Contact in case of difficulties

Derivation
- Installation and Conversion strategy
- System test experience
- Acceptance test experience

Format/Presentation
- Site standards

Quality Criteria
- Tested out by someone unfamiliar with the product
- The package contains all information required by someone not familiar with the product to install and operate it
- The tests cover all interfaces
- Training material covers all features.

Quality Method
- Quality Review

B 2.16Installation Guide

Purpose

To provide full instructions to those who will install and test the system. It is part of the Release Package and should be read in conjunction with it.

Composition

- System overview
- Instructions on any back-ups to be taken
- Installation instructions
- Installation test instructions
- Installation test data
- Installation test data expected results
- Possible error situations and their recovery
- Conversion instructions

Derivation

- Installation and conversion strategy

Format/Presentation

- Site standards

Quality Criteria

- Consistent with the installation and conversion strategy
- Covers all data to be captured and/or converted
- Clear to someone who does not know the product.

Quality Method

- Quality Review

B 2.17 Education Strategy

Purpose

To identify staff who will require training in the new system, and the different levels of training needed. It should cover the training of future as well as existing staff.

Composition

- Audience definitions
- Objectives for each level of audience
- Training methods
- Course syllabii and duration

- Schedule
- Resource requirements and responsibilities

Derivation
- Requirements Specification

Format/Presentation
- Site standards

Quality Criteria
- Every level of staff affected by the new system is covered
- The training modules will not mix groups
- The objectives have been agreed with each level of audience
- The methods chosen are suitable
- The schedule meets the operational needs
- The resource needs and responsibilities are agreed.

Quality Method
- Quality Review

B 2.18 Education Specification

Purpose
To identify the staff who require training, and specify the content and method for each type of training needed.

Composition
- The different groups of staff needing training
- Any assumptions which can be made about the background knowledge of each group
- The method of training each group
- The timescale for production of the material
- The recommended duration of each course or module
- Any testing requirements to be built into the courses
- The content to be covered by each course
- Any hardware or software to be used in the training
- The title and location of any products to be used as the basis for the material
- Quality Control points during the development of the material
- Contact names for questions.

Derivation
- Education Strategy

- Physical design
- User Assurance Co-ordinator

Format/Presentation
- Site standards

Quality Criteria
- Covers every user interface with the system
- Has both overview and detailed levels
- Has separate training for each different type of user
- Has hands-on training for the detailed levels wherever possible
- Has considered the need to test attendees and insist on a pass level or retake of the education

Quality Method
- Quality Review

B 2.19 Education Guide

Purpose
Contains the material and instructions to train all levels of staff to be affected by the product.

Composition
- To a certain extent the composition will depend on the specific strategy chosen. Below are listed some of the possibilities.
- Overview of the objectives and methods
- Levels of training and their audiences, plus any sequence information
- Pre-requisite knowledge and/or experience for each level
- Course syllabuses
- Timetables
- Lecturer notes
- Overhead foils
- Student notes
- Exercises and sample solutions@bullett = Case studies
- Practice data
- Expected results
- Computer based training material
- Foreign language translations
- Overviews

Derivation
- Education Specification

- exercises/workshops plus sample solutions

Format/Presentation
- Site standards

Quality Criteria
- Needs of each audience level covered
- Should any of the modules include a test to prove student competence?
- Assumptions of prior knowledge reasonable
- Covers all functions and procedures of the product.

Quality Method
- Quality Review

B 2.20 Trained Users

Purpose
To manage, use, control operate and maintain the system.

Composition
- Management
- Users
- Staff who interface with the system
- Maintenance staff

Derivation
- The training material
- Training courses

Format/Presentation
- Not applicable

Quality Criteria
- The staff have sufficient knowledge and skill to manage and operate the system
- Evidence that the staff have received the appropriate training
- Evidence that procedures and materials exist to train new staff.

Quality Method
- The users have reached a satisfactory pass mark in the education

B 2.21 User Guide

Purpose
To describe to users how to use the product.

Composition
- Overview
- System flow diagram
- Organisational requirements
- Interface descriptions
- Security arrangements
- How to obtain/create/change a password
- How to use the system
- How to log on
- How to log off
- How to enter data
- Standard use of function keys
- Action in case of run-time problems
- Error messages
- Identification and meaning
- Corrective action
- Index of functions
- Description of each function
- Purpose
- When used
- Preparation
- Forms to be used
- How invoked
- Special use of function keys
- Steps
- Screen display samples
- Otput samples
- Glossary of terms
- Cross-reference index

Derivation
- Physical system design

Format/Presentation
- Site standards

Quality Criteria
- Offers a complete and unambiguous step-by-step guide to the execu-

tion of every function and procedure
- Covers every function and procedure of the product
- Covers form use and filling
- Explains who does what
- Explanation of all possible product errors and recovery from them
- Easy to reference by function
- The product can be used from the instructions in the guide
- Has the method for updating the manual been decided?

Quality Method
- Quality Review

B 2.22 User Consumables

Purpose
To provide the user with any materials required by the system which are to be regularly consumed and are specific to that system. Examples are pre-printed stationery, floppy disks.

Composition
This depends on the type of consumable. Normally part of the composition will identify the specific system, such as the form heading and reference number. With floppy disks there may be a need for labels identifying the system. An example here would be a software house needing to identify the disks containing its product.

Derivation
- Physical design
- User procedures
- installation strategy

Format/Presentation
- Site standards

Quality Criteria
- Identify the system and the consumable's use
- Contain a reference number to identify the consumable and its version
- Contain adequate space for any information to be contained
- Advertise the product and company in a manner satisfactory to sales and marketing needs if it is to be seen externally
- Is of a material suitable for the user's purpose.

Quality Method
- Quality Review

B 2.23 User Procedures

Purpose

To provide instructions and guidance to users to enable them to carry out any manual procedure required by the system.

Composition
- Identification of the procedure
- Information on when and under what circumstances the procedure is required
- Identification of who should or is entitled to carry it out
- Reference to any authorisation needed
- List of any pre-requisites
- Description of the steps
- Identification of any possible errors which may be encountered whilst carrying out the procedure and the appropriate recovery actions
- Name of the contact in case further advice is needed
- Index of procedures
- Any necessary information about the interdependence of any procedures or their interaction with machine procedures

Derivation
- Physical Design

Format/Presentation
- Site standards

Quality Criteria
- Contain all the information required to successfully complete the procedure
- Cover all possible situations
- Cover all possible errors and recoveries from them
- Identify all the people to be involved and their responsibilities
- Are written in a language suitable for the users involved

Quality Method
- Quality Review

B 2.24 Operations Guide

Purpose
To describe the product to operations staff, giving full operating instructions and recovery procedures.

Composition
- Operations overview
- Description of operating environment
- Hardware
- Software
- Communications
- Hardware usage diagram
- Location of files on physical devices
- Interface descriptions
- Run descriptions
- Identity
- Run summary
- Scheduling
- Job preparation
- Source of input
- Format of input
- Samples of input
- Method of data input
- Security instructions
- Run stream example
- Parameter notes
- Secial instructions
- Completion procedures
- Output summary
- Output distribution
- Restart, rerun and phase selection
- Error conditions
- Recovery actions
- User contact
- Housekeeping
- File identification, usage and release
- Security and file recovery procedures

Derivation
- Physical system design

Format/Presentation
- Site standards

Quality Criteria
- Consistent with the way in which the system needs to work
- Covers errors and restarts
- Written in terms understandable by operations
- Acceptable to the operations staff.

Quality Method
- Quality Review

B 2.25 Hardware Environment

Purpose
Description of the equipment needed to run the system.

Composition
- Computer mode
- Memory requirement
- On-line storage requirement
- Peripheral requirements with any options

Derivation
- Terms of Reference
- Physical system design

Format/Presentation
- Site standards

Quality Criteria
- Within the constraints of the Terms of Reference
- Matches the needs of the physical system design
- A service level agreement has been reached.

Quality Method
- Quality Review

B 2.26 Trained Operators

Purpose
To operate the system.

Composition
- Trained operators

Derivation
- The training material
- Training courses

Format/Presentation
- Not applicable

Quality Criteria
- The operators have sufficient knowledge and skill to operate the system
- The operators have sufficient knowledge and skill to restore the system after a failure
- Evidence that the operators have received the appropriate training
- Evidence that procedures and materials exist to train new operators.

Quality Method
Quality Review

B 2.27 Operating Software

Purpose
Description of the operating system required to run the system.

Composition
- Name and version number of the operating system required
- List of any specific patches which must be applied to the operating system in order for the run time software to perform correctly
- Name and version number of any required telecommunications software required

Derivation
- Physical System Design
- System Test observations

Format/Presentation
- Site standards

Quality Criteria
- Must match with the software environment used for system test.

Quality Method
- Quality Review

B 2.28 Run Time Software

Purpose
To perform the functions described in the System Design.

Composition
- Machine-readable object and load modules
- Job Control Language/Batch Commands
- Data

Derivation
- System Design
- Programming

Format/Presentation
- Site standards

Quality Criteria
- Performs all the functions specified in the design documents
- Performs correctly and accurately
- Handles error situations and, where possible carries on
- Terminates in a controlled fashion with appropriate error messages when faced with irrecoverable error situations
- Departmental naming and coding standards have been used

Quality Method
- Quality Review

B 2.29 Operations Consumables

Purpose
To assist in the preparation, creation and distribution of the system data.

Composition
- Data preparation forms
- Batch forms
- Pre-printed stationery
- Listing paper
- Floppy disks
- Magnetic tapes (back-up)

Derivation
- Physical System Design
- Operations Guide

Format/Presentation
- Site standards

Quality Criteria
- No scraps of paper needed by staff inputting to the system
- All output identified as coming from the system
- System can be run and backed up over several cycles from the consumables provided
- Matches all consumables mentioned in the Operations Guide.

Quality Method
- Quality Review

B3 Quality Products

B 3.1 Product Descriptions

Purpose
To describe a product in sufficient detail that it can be created and later checked for content and quality.

Composition
- Unique identifier
- Purpose
- Composition
- Derivation
- Format/Presentation
- Quality Criteria
- External Dependencies

Derivation
- PRINCE manual (or this book)
- Site standards
- Project specifics

Format/Presentation
- This is it

Quality Criteria
- Describes fully the composition of the product
- Explains how to measure the quality of the product
- Describes from where the information is to come.

Quality Method
- Quality Review

B 3.2 Quality File

Purpose

The Quality File contains the forms which are produced as part of the quality controls of the project, and can be used by an external body to audit the function and use of those controls.

Composition

The file should have sections for each of the following forms:
- Quality Review Log
- Quality Review Invitation
- Quality Review Result Notification
- Quality Review Action List
- Technical Exception and Exception Memo Log
- Exception Memo
- Project Issue Report
- Request For Change

Derivation
- The sections of the file are created during Project Initiation.
- The contents are derived from the creation of the forms mentioned above.

Format/Presentation
- Site standards

Quality Criteria
- When processing of a form is complete, the original of the form should be held in the file
- All forms should have a unique reference number which matches the log
- The logs should be up-to-date
- For each entry on the logs, a copy of the form must be in the appropriate section.

B 3.3 Quality Review Invitation

Purpose

To confirm the date, venue, time and subject of a Quality Review to all attendees.

Composition

- Title/Purpose of the document
- Date
- Recipient's name, job title and location
- Sender's name, location, telephone and/or fax number
- Subject – identity of the product to be reviewed
- Date, time, venue and expected duration of the review
- List of the attendees and their roles
- Copy of the product (not for BAC or presenter)
- Copy of the product description
- Checklist (if applicable)
- Identification of standards applicable to the product
- Blank question list
- Final date for return of Question List
- Request for acknowledgement

Derivation

- Quality plan
- List of reviewers agreed by chairman, Project Assurance Team and presenter

Format/Presentation

- See form sample in Appendix E.

Quality Criteria

- Contains all the information listed above
- Is distributed with sufficient warning that the reviewers have time to study the product and arrange their diaries

B 3.4 Quality Review Follow Up Action List

Purpose

To list the actions decided upon at a Quality Review together with dates and responsibilities for doing the work.

Composition

- Title/Purpose of the document

- Date
- Quality Review number
- Title and identity of the product reviewed
- Annotated product
- List of agreed actions
- Per action:
     who is to take the action
     target date for the work
     who is to check the result of the action
     Chairman's signature

Derivation
- Quality review discussions
- Quality review standard

Format/Presentation
- See form sample in Appendix E.

Quality Criteria
- Lists every further action required
- Each action item has been read back to the reviewers during the review and agreed
- Someone has been appointed to action each point
- At least one person has been appointed to check the result of each action
- A target date has been agreed for each action.

Quality Method
- Quality Review

B 3.5 Quality Review Result Notification

Purpose
To confirm the result of the review to the stage manager and attendees of the review.

Composition
- Title/Purpose of the document
- Quality review number and product identity
- Date of the review
- Indication of whether the review was complete or incomplete
- Summary of the result/reasons for the status decision
- (if incomplete) Action recommended, which should be one of:

re-work the product and reconvene the review
reconvene without re-work (ran out of time)
reconvene with a different set of reviewers
treat the product as complete after re-work of errors found
   so far
abandon the review and accept the product as is
- Chairman's signature

Derivation
- Action list from the review
- Consensus of chairman, reviewers and presenter

Format/Presentation
- See form sample in Appendix E.

Quality Criteria
- Uniquely identifies the pertinent quality review
- Clarifies the review result
- Provides sufficient data for the Stage Manager to know the product's completeness and quality
- Is sent to every reviewer, the presenter and BAC.

B 3.6 Project Issue Report

Purpose
To document a desired addition or change to the Requirements Specification or a current failure to meet it or the Acceptance Criteria.

Composition
- Project
- Date and log number
- Status
- Author
- Description of the issue
- Analysis of the products affected and the effort to do the work
- Forecast cost of the change
- Decision
- Cross-reference to any Request For Change or Off-specification raised as a result of the issue

Derivation
- Ideas for improvement
- Perceived failures to meet specification (outside those identified in the

product quality review)
- Management issues such as potential problems
- Inconsistencies between versions of a Configuration Item

Format/Presentation
- See form sample in Appendix E.

Quality Criteria
- Complete and accurate statement of the issue
- Assessed by a member of the Project Assurance Team
- Logged by the Configuration Librarian
- Copy passed to the originator.

Quality Method
- Quality Review

B 3.7 Off-Specification Report

Purpose
To document any situation where a product fails to meet its specification

Composition
- Date
- Log number
- Class
- Status
- Cross-reference to its associated Project Issue Report
- Description of the fault
- Impact of the fault
- Priority assessment
- Decision
- Allocation details,if applicable
- Date allocated
- Date completed

Derivation
- Project Issue Report

Format/Presentation
- See form sample in Appendix E.

Quality Criteria
- Logged by the Configuration Librarian

- Cross-referenced to the originating Project Issue Report
- Accurate transcription of the issue
- Reviewed regularly by the Project Manager and Project Assurance Team until closed.

B 3.8 Request For Change

Purpose
To request a modification to the product as currently specified.

Composition
- Date
- Logged number
- Class
- Status
- Cross-reference to the originating Project Issue Report
- Description of the proposed change
- Impact of the change
- Priority assessment
- Decision
- Allocation details
- Date allocated
- Date completed

Derivation
- Project Issue Report

Format/Presentation
- See form sample in Appendix E.

Quality Criteria
- Logged by the Configuration Librarian
- Cross-referenced to the originating Project Issue Report
- Accurate transcription of the issue
- Reviewed regularly by the Project Manager and Project Assurance Team until closed.

Appendix C Organisation Roles

Figure C.1 shows again the roles defined by PRINCE for a project, and standard job descriptions follow for each role. Remember that roles can be shared or combined, depending on the individual project circumstances.

The standard descriptions are based on the information contained in the NCC Blackwell PRINCE Guides. They are based on an IT project, but you will notice that only small changes would be required for a non-IT project.

The Project Board

The Project Board has the overall responsibility for delivering the required system. It is the ultimate project authority and is responsible for the initiation, monitoring and review and eventual closure of the project. To meet this function, Project Board members must be of managerial level with the appropriate level of authority necessary to commit the resources required by the project.

Role Summary
1. Provide overall direction and guidance to the project based on the brief passed down from the IT Executive Committee.
2. Obtain the IT Executive Committee decision or endorsement in any circumstances where the overall strategy, its milestones or justification are threatened or when changes in policy appear necessary.
3. Commit the necessary resources to carry out the project.
4. Ensure that the project meets agreed standards of quality, time and cost.
5. Ensure that the project remains viable against its Business Case.
6. Have ultimate project responsibility and authority for the quality of the products, responsible to the company or department executive who is in overall charge of quality.

Specific Activities
1. Appoint the Project Manager, Project Assurance Team and any Stage Managers required.
2. Ensure that terms of reference (a Project Brief) are available and

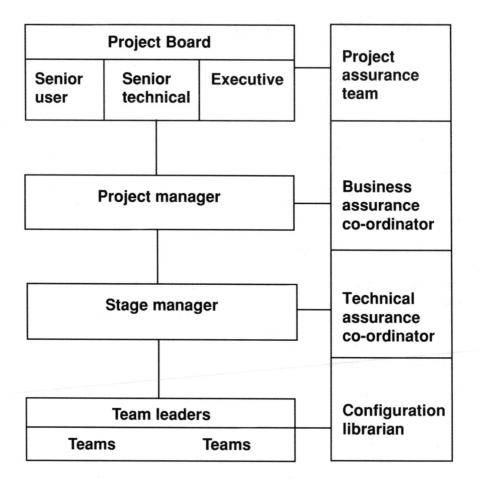

Figure C.1 PRINCE Organisation Roles

     understood by the project management team.
3.   Check and approve the Project Initiation Document.
4.   Review and approve all project and stage plans.
5.   Ensure that a quality strategy has been developed which is in line with the Project Brief, and that quality plans exist for the project and in detail for each stage.
6.   Set tolerance levels for each plan.
7.   Authorise the start of each stage, or recommend termination of the project.

8. Monitor plan progress at a frequency decided by them.
9. Make decisions on any Exception Plan presented to them.
10. Ensure that all products are complete and delivered at the end of each stage.
11. Approve the Project Evaluation Review.
12. Authorise project closure.
13. Report back to the ITEC.

The Project Board consists of representatives from three functional areas:

Executive.   Prime Responsibility: to ensure that the system under development achieves the expected benefits and that the project is completed within guidelines provided by the ITEC.

Senior User.   Prime Responsibility: to represent the interests of the user department(s) affected by the project, to monitor progress against the requirements of user management and to commit the user resources required by approved plans.

Senior Technical.   Prime Responsibility: to represent the interests of the development organisation (and operations if it is a computer project) and commit development resources required by approved plans.

The three roles comprising the Project Board should not be interpreted as a requirement for three individuals. In smaller projects roles may be combined in one person; in other circumstances several individuals may take on a single functional role (e.g. where a number of users areas are being served by the system development).

Executive

Role Summary
1. To ensure that the product being developed achieves the expected benefits.
2. To ensure that the project is completed within the costs and timescales approved by the IT Executive Committee.

Specific Activities
1. Organise and chair Project Board meetings.
2. Ensure that appointments are made and responsibilities defined for Project Manager, Stage Manager and the Project Assurance Team.
3. Authorise expenditure and agree tolerance levels for each stage plan.
4. Sign off project and stage plans.
5. Confirm that all plans meet policy and strategic needs.
6. Monitor the continuing viability of the project against the Business Case and the project's overall objectives.
7. Ensure that the project is provided at the outset with its business

objectives and project tolerance levels.
8. Understand:
   the overall IT strategy;
   the long-term strategy relevant to the project area;
   IT concepts;
   the PRINCE project management standard;
9. Report to the IT Executive Committee.

Senior User

Role Summary
1. To represent the interests of the user department(s) affected by the project.
2. To monitor progress against the requirements of user management.

Specific Activities
1. Agree objectives and quality criteria for products having a direct user impact.
2. Approve Product Descriptions for those products with a direct user impact.
3. Approve the User Specification and Acceptance Criteria.
4. Resolve priority conflicts in user requirements.
5. Assign and commit all user resources.
6. Sign off System Installation and Conversion plans.
7. Approve User Education plans.
8. Sign the User Acceptance Letter on successful completion of the system installation.
9. Brief and advise user management on all project matters.
10. Ensure that the User Assurance Co-ordinator is properly briefed to deal with day-to-day matters on behalf of the user(s).
11. Prioritise Requests For Change and make recommendations to the Project Board on the action to be taken on them. This includes the willingness to approve Exception Plans to implement the Requests For Change if they cannot be done within the Stage Plan tolerance.

Senior Technical

Role Summary
1. To represent the interests of the development organisation.
2. To represent, where appropriate, the interests of the operations organisation.

Specific Activities
1. Agree objectives for technical activities.
2. Approve Product Descriptions for technical products.
3. Assign technical resources needed by the project.
4. Arbitrate on and ensure the resolution of any technical priority or resource conflicts.
5. Sign off Project and Stage Technical Plans.
6. Prepare and sign the System Acceptance Letter on successful completion of system tests.
7. Brief non-technical management on any project technical aspects.
8. Ensure that the Technical Assurance Co-ordinator is properly briefed to deal with day-to-day problems.

The Project Manager

Large projects, or those involving multiple project development, need an additional level of control to co-ordinate the total development effort. The Project Manager fulfils this role.

The prime responsibility of the Project Manager is to ensure that the project as a whole produces the required products, to the required standard of quality, and within the specified constraints of time and cost.

It is the responsibility of the Project Manager to co-ordinate the efforts of all Stage Managers on all the projects associated with the system development under his control.

Role Summary
1. To ensure that the project as a whole produces the required products to the defined standard of quality.
2. To complete the project within cost and time constraints.

Specific Activities
1. Plan the project and agree the plan with the Project Board.
2. Liaise with associated/related projects.
3. Prepare Stage Plans.
4. Recommend a tolerance level for each stage plan.
5. Agree reporting frequency with the Project Board for each stage.
6. Define Stage Manager objectives and responsibilities.
7. Monitor overall project progress.
8. Advise the Project Board immediately plan tolerance levels are exceeded.
9. Prepare and present Exception Plans to the Project Board as required.
10. Collate the Checkpoint reports of the Stage Manager.
11. Send regular Highlight Reports to the Project Board.

12. Monitor the results of all control meetings held within the stage team.
13. Liaise with the Project Assurance Team to assure the overall integrity and direction of the project.
14. Attend all Mid-, End-Stage Assessments, Project Initiation and Closure meetings.
15. Agree the technical and quality strategy with the Project Board.
16. Agree configuration aspects with the Business Assurance Co-ordinator and Configuration Librarian.

Stage Manager

Role Summary
1.   To ensure production of the stage products to the required quality.
2.   To meet stage cost and time constraints.

Specific Activities
1.   Assist the Project Manager in the preparation of the stage to be managed.
2.   Define objectives, responsibilities and work plans for Stage Teams and Team Leaders.
3.   Manage and provide guidance to Team Leaders.
4.   Monitor progress and resource utilisation.
5.   Initiate corrective action where necessary.
6.   Ensure all technical Exceptions are reported, evaluated and corrective action instigated.
7.   Attend the End-Stage and any Mid-Stage Assessments of the stage managed.
8.   Attend the End-Stage Assessment of the previous stage.
9.   Attend Checkpoint meetings where possible.
10. Liaise with the Project Assurance Team to ensure the business, technical and data integrity of the stage.
11. Advise the Project Manager of any Exception Planning necessary.
12. Ensure that Quality Reviews are held as planned.
13. Ensure the maintenance of the Stage File.
14. Advise and support the Project Manager in deciding on corrective action.
15. Prepare and present regular Checkpoint reports to the Project Manager.

Project Assurance Team

The Project Assurance Team (PAT) comprises the following functional responsibilities:

- The Business Assurance Co-ordinator (BAC)
- The Technical Assurance Co-ordinator (TAC)
- The User Assurance Co-ordinator (UAC)
- The Configuration Librarian (CL)

Role Summary
1. To provide support and assurance to the Project Board, Project and Stage Managers.
2. To support the Team Leaders and members in terms of advice and interpretation of project management, quality and technical standards.

Specific Activities
1. Help the Project Manager to prepare plans.
2. Co-ordinate all Quality Review activities.
3. Assist in monitoring and recording actuals.
4. Attend stage assessment meetings.
5. Attend team Checkpoint meetings.
6. Advise the Project Manager of any plan deviations.
7. Assess the impact of Technical Exceptions.
8. Advise the Project Board on product status and acceptability.
9. Liaise with the development team to ensure that user requirements are being met.
10. Advise the development teams on user requirements.
11. Offer advice and guidance to members of the development team on use of the relevant technical standards.

The Business Assurance Co-ordinator
The Business Assurance Co-ordinator's main tasks revolve around helping the Project Manager (and Stage Managers, if the role is used) to prepare, agree, distribute and update the plans. In particular the Business Assurance Co-ordinator is responsible for producing the resource plans from information supplied by the Project and Stage Managers and Technical Assurance Co-ordinator.

In addition the Business Assurance Co-ordinator will co-ordinate all Quality Review activities and assure the Quality Management standards for the project. Where there is no separate Configuration Librarian role allocated within the Project Assurance Team, the Business Assurance Co-ordinator will assume the bulk of the Configuration Librarian's responsibilities.

Role Summary
1. To assist in all resource planning and monitor and report on cost and

resource utilisation.
2. To act as focal point for administrative controls.

Specific Activities
1. Help the Project Manager to prepare the Project Resource Plans.
2. Help the Project Manager to prepare the Stage Resource Plans at the end of each stage and ensure compatibility with the Project Resource Plan.
3. Prepare Detailed Resource Plans with the Stage Manager.
4. Liaise with the Technical Assurance Co-ordinator to ensure consistency between Technical and Resource plans.
5. Co-ordinate all PRINCE Quality Review activities.
6. Co-ordinate all Technical Exception activities.
7. Perform Configuration Audit Reviews.
8. Collect actual resource usage data and record against the plan.
9. Translate resource usage into actual costs.
10. Monitor actual usage against plan and advise the Stage Manager of deviations.
11. Attend Checkpoint meetings where possible.
12. Assist the Stage Manager to prepare Checkpoint reports.
13. Assist the Project Manager to prepare Highlight Reports.
14. Attend and minute all Mid- and End-Stage Assessments.
15. Provide costs and resourcing data to any Exception Plans required.
16. Establish and maintain the project Quality File.
17. Have a thorough knowledge of any project planning software to be used.

Technical Assurance Co-ordinator (TAC)
The Technical Assurance Co-ordinator provides technical support and advice to the Project Board, Project Manager, Stage Managers, Team Leaders and Team Members. The individual(s) filling this role may change as the project moves through different stages, needing different technical skills.

Role Summary
1. To plan, monitor and report on all technical assurance aspects of the project.
2. To ensure correct use of technical standards defined for the project.

Specific Activities
1. Help the Project Manager to prepare the Project Technical Plan.
2. Help the Project Manager to prepare Stage Technical Plans.
3. Prepare detailed Technical Plans as required by the Stage Manager.

4. Liaise with the Business Assurance Co-ordinator to ensure a match between technical and resource plans.
5. Assist Project/Stage Managers to select appropriate technical strategies.
6. Assess new techniques/methods and report on their possible use in the project.
7. Advise on the applicability of current technical standards.
8. Attend Quality Reviews of technical products.
9. Verify overall system security and recovery procedures.
10. Monitor technical progress and advise the Stage Manager.
11. Attend Checkpoint meetings where possible.
12. Assist the Project Manager to produce Highlight Reports.
13. Assist in the preparation for Mid- and End-Stage Assessments.
14. Attend all Mid- and End-Stage Assessments.
15. Advise the Project Manager on technical aspects of Exception Plans.
16. Advise on the technical impact of Technical Exceptions.
17. Ensure that the Technical File is established and maintained.
18. Advise the Project Board (especially Senior Technical) as required about technical status.

User Assurance Co-ordinator (UAC)

The User Assurance Co-ordinator provides the day-to-day link between the technical developers and the users.

The User Assurance Co-ordinator should ideally be located with the Business Assurance Co-ordinator and Technical Assurance Co-ordinator but is more likely to be carrying out the User Assurance Co-ordinator tasks within his normal work.

The prime responsibilities of the User Assurance Co-ordinator are to:

- Understand the work and methods of the user area affected by the project and be able to advise on the current system and new user requirements
- monitor the team work to ensure that user requirements are being understood and a solution developed which will meet those needs.

Role Summary
1. To monitor and report on all user-related aspects of the project.
2. To represent the user on a day-to-day basis.

Specific Activities
1. Ensure that User Specifications are correct, complete, unambiguous and agreed by users.
2. Ensure the correct identification of all user products.

3. Ensure that all user requirementsare produced in the relevant plans.
4. Input any user job descriptions required into the User Specification.
5. Ensure the establishment of User Acceptance Criteria.
6. Write the Product Descriptions for all user products.
7. Advise on which users should attend any Quality Reviews.
8. Provide test data and expected results for User Acceptance Tests.
9. Verify system security and recovery procedures from a user point-of-view.
10. Ensure that the project gathers, maintains, protects and distributes data in a manner acceptable to the user.
11. Attend those Quality Reviews where user verification is required.
12. Attend Checkpoint meetings where possible.
13. Provide input for the preparation of Checkpoint and Highlight Reports.
14. Help prepare for and attend all Mid- and End-Stage Assessments.
15. Provide the assessment of user impact for any Technical Exceptions.
16. Provide assessment of the user impact for any Exception Plans.

Configuration Librarian (CL)

The Configuration Librarian is the custodian of all master copies of the project's products. The role also includes the maintenance of the Technical Exception files.

Role Summary
1. To supply a method supporting the labelling, receipt, issue, storage and status control of all project products.
2. Interface between the project and the Configuration Management Method.
3. To log, store and distribute Technical Exceptions.

Specific Activities
1. Assist the Project Manager to prepare the Configuration Management Plan.
2. Create a coding scheme to label all products.
3. Create libraries to hold all products.
4. Assist in the identification of Configuration Items (CI).
5. Create Configuration Item Description Records (CIDR).
6. Accept and record receipt of Submission Request Forms with new or revised products into the CM library.
7. Archive superseded Configuration data.
8. Act as custodian for master copies of all project products.
9. Issue product copies for review, change, correction or information.
10. Maintain issue logs for both human and machine readable products.

11. Notify holders of any changes to their copies.
12. Maintain logs for Project Issue Reports, Requests For Change and Off-Specifications.
13. Monitor all Technical Exception documents and ensure they are re-submitted to the CM library after authorised change.
14. Assist the Technical Assurance Co-ordinator to assess the impact of a change to a CI.
15. Produce Configuration Status Accounting reports.
16. Assist in conducting Configuration Audits.
17. Liaise with other librarians where products are common to other systems.

PRINCE Co-ordinator

Role Summary
1. To act as internal consultant for PRINCE project control procedures.
2. To ensure the smooth introduction and continuing effective use of the PRINCE methodology.

Specific Activities
1. To develop expertise in PRINCE so that the site can become self-sufficient in terms of support.
2. To act as the Business Assurance Co-ordinator on an initial PRINCE project.
3. To administer and monitor the implementation of PRINCE to ensure that it meets the needs of the site and its departments.
4. To ensure that the methodology continues to be used in accordance with agreed standards.
5. To make managers who might be involved in future projects aware of the methodology and ensure that proper consideration is given to its use.
6. To identify PRINCE training needs at all levels of the organisation.
7. To plan, organise and present detailed training and management overviews.
8. To liaise with the PRINCE User Group, disseminating any enhancements or practical experience from other users.
9. To act as focal point for requests for change to the methodology or documentation.
10. To liaise with the CCTA on any received requests for change to the methodology.

Project Support Office

A central Project Support Office within a company or department may provide staff for the Project Assurance Team, particularly the PRINCE Co-ordinator, Business Assurance Co-ordinator and Configuration Librarian. In a working environment with a limited number of techniques and technical standards, sometimes the Technical Assurance Co-ordinator role can be supplied from a central group. But it is more likely that this role will be someone with the required skills who is working in another project. This person is seconded to work part-time in the other project as Technical Assurance Co-ordinator.

The Business Assurance Co-ordinator role can be approached in a number of ways. It is possible for one BAC to act for several small projects at the same time. It is also possible in a large organisation for a senior BAC to operate at the level of the IT Steering Committee and organise multi-project reports, resource summaries and so on.

Appendix D Activity Lists

Project Initiation Activities

Attendees
Project Board
Project Manager
Stage Manager for the first stage
Project Assurance Team
PRINCE Co-ordinator (if appropriate)

Activity	Responsible
Preparation	
Establish initial project scope and boundary	ITEC
1. Appoint Project Board and define their responsibilities.	ITEC
2. Agree and refine project scope and boundary with related projects.	ITEC
3. Define project business objectives.	ITEC
4. Appoint Project Manager and define responsibilities.	Executive
5. Appoint first stage manager and define responsibilities.	Executive
6. Appoint Project Assurance Team and define responsibilities.	PB
7. Establish availability of resources for project.	PM/BAC
8. Appoint members of first Stage Team.	PM/SM
9. Ensure that a Configuration Management System is established.	PM/CL
10. Ensure that relationships with other projects are documented.	PB
11. Ensure that the Project Brief is adequate.	PB
12. Ensure that the list of products is complete.	PB
13. Ensure that any requirement for an IT Security Risk Analysis and Management Review is included in the Project Brief.	PB
14. Create the Project File.	

	PM
15. Create the Quality File.	BAC
16. Create the Technical File.	TAC
17. Assess the risk that the project will not be completed on time and to budget.	PM
18. Prepare Project Technical Plans.	PM/TAC
19. Prepare Project Resource Plans.	PM/BAC
20. Prepare Stage Technical Plans for first stage.	PM/TAC
21. Prepare Stage Resource Plans for first stage.	PM/BAC
22. Organise Project Initiation Meeting.	PM/BAC
23. Study all documents circulated and prepare questions.	Attendees

Review

24. Review and agree management structure and individual responsibilities.	Executve
25. Review project objectives.	PB
26. Approve Project Plan.	PB
27. Approve first Stage Plan.	PB
28. Define the number of stages, frequency of Checkpoints and Highlight Reports, and any Mid-Stage Assessments to be held.	PB
29. Confirm that the level of authority of the Project Board members is commensurate with the project scope.	Executive
30. Ensure that the measures recommended to meet the business risks to successful completion are acceptable.	PB
31. Approve Project Initiation Document.	PB

Stage Management Activities

Activities at the Start of a Stage

1. Create the Stage File.	Stage Manager
2. Prepare Individual Work Plans.	Stage Manager
3. Identify technical training needs.	Stage Manager /TAC
4. Plan technical training.	Stage Manager /TAC

Activities During a Stage

1. Maintain Quality File.	BAC
2. Maintain Stage File.	Stage Manager

	/BAC
3. Update Stage Technical Plan.	Stage Manager
	/TAC
4. Update Stage Resource Plan.	Stage Manager
	/BAC
5. Hold Checkpoint Meetings.	Stage Manager
	/BAC/TAC
6. Prepare Checkpoint Reports	Stage Manager
	/BAC/TAC
7. Prepare Highlight Reports.	Project Manager
8. Ensure Quality Reviews are held and reported.	Stage Manager
	/BAC
9. Log Project Issue Reports.	Config Librarian
10. Assess technical impact of PIR's.	TAC/Config Librarian
11. Make recommendations on PIR's.	Stage Manager
	/PAT
12. Make decisions on PIR's.	Project Manager
13. Progress Off-Specifications andRequests for Change	Project Manager /Stage Manager /PAT
14. Prepare any Exception Plans needed.	Project Manager /Stage Manager /PAT
15. Prepare any Mid-Stage Assessments.	Project Manager
16. Hold any Mid-Stage Assessments needed.	Project Board

Activities at the End of a Stage

1. Bring current Stage Plans up-to-date.	Stage Manager /PAT
2. Assess impact of current stage actuals on Project Plans.	Project Manager /PAT
3. Prepare Stage Technical Plan for next stage.	Project Manager /TAC /next StageManager
4. Prepare Stage Resource Plan for next stage.	Project Manager /BAC /next Stage Manager
5. Document next stage plan description, assumptions, risks and pre-requisites.	Project manager
6. Assess impact of next Stage Plan on Project Plan.	Project Manager /BAC

7. Revise Project Business Case figures.	Project Manager /BAC
8. Prepare for End-Stage Assessment.	Project Board
9. Prepare report to End-Stage Assessment.	Project Manager /BAC/TAC/UAC
10. Hold End-Stage Assessment.	Project Board
11. Set tolerance level and reporting frequency.	Project Board
12. Prepare Approval to Proceed form.	Project Manager
13. Sign Approval to Proceed form.	Project Board
14. Prepare report to IT Executive	Executive on PB Committee

Activities at the Project Closure Meeting
1.   Check that all required Configuration Items are complete and delivered.
2.   Ensure that the status of all outstanding Requests For Change and Off-Specifications is documented.
3.   Check that all Project Issue Reports have been closed.
4.   Prepare a Project Evaluation Review.
5.   Ensure that IT security requirements have been incorporated and signed off.
6.   Prepare for Project Closure meeting.
7.   Hold Project Closure meeting.
8.   Verify that System, User and Operations Acceptance Letters have been signed off.
9.   Arrange for a Post Implementation Review of the system when the data files have been built up and the system tuned.
10. Establish timing for next IT Security Risk Analysis.
11. Write Business Acceptance Letter to the IT Executive Committee.
12. If the circumstances demand it, the Executive also writes a Security Acceptance Letter to the IT Executive Committee, describing the IT security measures which have been implemented for the system.

Quality Review Activities
1.   The chairman confirms with the presenter that the product will be finished by the planned date. If there is a delay, the chairman writes an Exception Memo to the Business Assurance Co-ordinator, stating the new planned finish date. The Business Assurance Co-ordinator updates the Technical Plan and informs the Stage Manager.
2.   The chairman and presenter produce a list of required attendees, and decide if the product's complexity is such that a presentation to explain it to the reviewers before they do their preparation is required.
3.   The chairman sets up the venue, time and date and makes out

invitations for the attendees.
4. The invitations are passed to the Configuration Librarian who adds a copy of the product to be reviewed, updating the Configuration Item Description Records. The presenter does not need a copy of the product.
5. The documents are passed to the Business Assurance Co-ordinator who adds copies of the Product Description and any relevant checklist. From the Quality Review log a unique identifier is added to the invitation. The package is then passed to each attendee.
6. The reviewers examine the product. Any grammatical errors are annotated on the product copy. A Question List is created of anything which is unclear or which is suspected to be an error. This should be done sufficiently early that the Question List and annotated copy can be passed back to the chairman in time for an agenda for the review to be made out. If a reviewer finds it impossible to attend the review, the Question List must still be made out and passed with the annotated copy to the chairman before the review.
7. On receipt of the Question Lists the chairman and presenter examine them and make out an agenda for the meeting. This includes prioritising the questions and making a rough time allocation to each.
8. If the review is delayed beyond the planned date, the chairman sends an Exception Memo to the Business Assurance Co-ordinator with the revised data. The Business Co-ordinator updates the Technical Plan and informs the Stage Manager.
9. The Business Assurance Co-ordinator files a copy of the invitation in the Quality File.

Review
1. The chairman introduces the review, stating its objectives, reminding the attendees of the time available, advising the attendees of any format for the review and tendering apologies for any non-attendees.
2. If the chairman feels that an adequate review cannot be held because of the absence of key reviewers, it can be declared incomplete. In such a case, all the documents are passed to the Business Assurance Co-ordinator with an Exception Memo containing a recommendation of action to be sent on to the Stage Manager.
3. If the presenter has seen the Question Lists in advance and feels there is a general misunderstanding of the product, a brief clarification can be made here. The aim is to avoid wasting time when dealing with the questions. The chairman should be aware of the danger of a lot of time being lost by the presenter losing sight of the need to be brief, and launching into a lot of self-justification. The presenter can suggest the need for this clarification, but it should be the chairman's decision on

whether it is needed.

4.   If the chairman has not seen the Question Lists in advance, there will be no knowledge of how many questions are to be asked, nor of what severity. In this case, the chairman should go round each reviewer and ask them to read out their questions. These should be consolidated on a list which everyone can see, for example, on a flipchart. The chairman should at this time allow no expansion or discussion on the question and no answer from the presenter. The only purpose is to make an agenda.

5.   If, on seeing the list, the chairman feels that the errors in the product are such that it is pointless to continue, the review can be declared incomplete and all documents sent to the Business Co-ordinator with the chairman's recommendation.

6.   The chairman selects the sequence of questions. The reviewer who raised it is asked for any necessary expansion, and the presenter asked to comment. The chairman controls the discussion, making sure that everyone with a worthwhile contribution has a chance to make it. The purpose is to discover whether there is an error in the product or not. The chairman has to ensure that no attempt is made to redesign the product and the presenter does not become defensive about the product. If there is a disagreement which cannot be resolved, the chairman has to avoid time being wasted by the repetition of arguments. The item in question should be made an action point for the appropriate people to settle outside the review.

7.   When an action point is identified, this must be noted. This is done by either the chairman or, if appointed, the scribe. If a scribe is being used, the chairman has the task of giving the scribe enough time to write down the action point before the next question is decided. After a number of actions have been raised, it is a useful practice for the chairman to ask the scribe to read out the points so far for the reviewers to confirm that no point has been missed or documented incorrectly.

8.   At the end of the review, the chairman reads back, or asks the scribe to do so, the agreed actions. For each action the person or people who will take the corrective action is (or are) identified. Usually this will be the presenter. A target date for each action is set. This should be as soon as possible and should take priority over any new work the person taking action is doing. An absolute maximum of five days is recommended. For each action, one or more of the reviewers must be appointed to confirm that the correction has solved the problem and not created any new ones.

9.   The final task for the chairman is to decide on the result of the review. This can be:

- the product is error-free
- the product will be error-free when the Follow Up Action List tasks have been done
- there are too many errors and/or omissions in the product to guarantee that a few action points will make it error-free.

10. If the result is the latter, all the documents are passed to the Business Assurance Co-ordinator.
11. If the review can be declared complete (error-free or with a few correctable errors), the Follow-Up Action List, Question Lists and annotated product copies are passed to the presenter. For safety a copy of the Action List should be given to the Business Assurance Co-ordinator.
12. The chairman makes out a Result Notification, indicating whether the review was complete or not. Copies of this go to the presenter, reviewers and the Business Assurance Co-ordinator.
13. If the review was incomplete, the Business Assurance Co-ordinator updates the Technical Plan and passes all the documentation to the Stage Manager for a decision.
14. If the review was complete, the Business Assurance Co-ordinator files the Result Notification in the Quality File.

Follow-Up

1. If a product is required urgently and there is insufficient time to correct an error, that error can be transferred to a Project Issue Report. This action should be used with care and requires the Project Manager's approval. The Follow Up Action List should be annotated with the Project Issue Report number.
2. The person (normally the presenter) or persons appointed resolve the points on the Follow-Up Action List
3. Once corrected, each action point is signed off by the person or persons appointed.
4. If the action points cannot be resolved within the time agreed, the chairman should be notified and an Exception Memo written to the Business Assurance Co-ordinator to keep the Technical Plan up-to-date.
5. On completion and sign-off of all the corrections, the Follow Up Action List is signed off by the chairman, and a copy sent to the Business Assurance Co-ordinator and all reviewers.
6. The Business Assurance Co-ordinator files the copy of the signed Follow Up Action List.
7. The re-worked product should be submitted to the Configuration Librarian.

Appendix E Sample Form Layouts

Title:	Checkpoint Report	Doc. No:	
Project:		Page	of
Stage:		Author:	

Report Period	From:	To:

Section 1: Activities Undertaken Since Last Report

Section 2: Objectives For Next Period

Figure E.1 Checkpoint report sample form

Title:	Highlight Report	Doc. No:	
Project:		Page	of
Stage:		Author:	

Report Period	From:	To:

Section 1: Activities Undertaken Since Last Report

Section 2: Objectives For Next Period

Summary of Progress		Spend				Schedule	
	Under	On Target	Over	Under	On Target	Over
Project: Stage:							

Figure E.2 Highlight Report

Title:	Sign-off Document	Doc. No:	
Project:		Page	of
Stage:		Author:	

Approved Signatures:	Function:
_____	_____
_____	_____
_____	_____
_____	_____
_____	_____
_____	_____

Comments:

The Project has formal approval to proceed to .... Stage.

Date of Approval .... Signature ....

Figure E.3 Sign-off document

Title:	Quality Review Invitation	Doc. No:
Project:		Page of
Stage:		Author:

To:
Branch/Address

From:
Branch/Address

Telephone:

You are invited to attend a Quality Review Meeting as a Reviewer.

End-Product Ref: Description:

Technical Guide/Standards Ref:

Venue:
Date: Time:

Chairman:
Presenter:
Reviewers:

Please provide Error Lists as soon as possible in advance of the Quality
Review Meeting -- in any case not later than:

Figure E.4 Quality review invitation

Title:	Quality Review Error List		Doc. No:	
Project:			Page	of
Stage:			Author:	

Ref. No.	Location	Comment	Cat.

Figure E.5 Quality Review error list

Title:	Q R Follow-up Action List	Doc. No:		
Project:		Page	of	
Stage:		Author:		

Ref. No.	Location/Description	I D	Signature

Figure E.6 QR Follow-up action list

Title:	Q R Results Notification	Doc. No:	
Project:		Page	of
Stage:		Author:	

The result of the Formal/Informal Quality Review for End-Product
Reference .... Description .... was:

Follow-up:		Estimated Completion:	
Re-Schedule:		Re-Schedule QR Date:	
Complete:			

Comments:

Reviewer's Sign-off

(Presenter)	
(Reviewer)	
(Reviewer)	
(Reviewer)	

Chairman's Comments:

Date: ....   Chairman's Signature ....

Figure E.7 QR Result notification

Project Issue

Project:	Stage:	P I R No:
Author:		Date:

Situation Description

Proposal for Resolution

Recommendation

Date: Appraised by:

Action		Date	
Action		Date	
Action		Date	
Action		Date	

Figure E.8 Project Issue

REQUEST FOR CHANGE

Project: Stage: R F C No:

Date: Associated P I R No:

Requested by: Priority:

Description:
Reason & Benifits:
Required date:
Technical evaluation:
Cost:

Action		Authorisation:	Date:	
Action		Authorisation:	Date:	
Action		Authorisation:	Date:	
Action		Authorisation:	Date:	
Action		Authorisation:	Date:	

Figure E.9 Request for change

OFF-SPECIFICATION REPORT

Project: Stage: O-SR No:

Date: Associated P I R No:

Off-specification Description:

Impact Analysis: Date:
Author:

Estimated Costs:
Author:

Action		Authorisation:	Date:	
Action		Authorisation:	Date:	
Action		Authorisation:	Date:	
Action		Authorisation:	Date:	
Action		Authorisation:	Date:	

Figure E.10 Off-specification report

Glossary

Acceptance Letters
There are four Acceptance Letters written during the final stages of a project:

- The System Acceptance Letter is signed by the Senior Technical member of the Project Board on successful completion of the System Test. It may be prepared by the Stage or Project Manager.
- The Operations Acceptance Letter is prepared by the Operations Manager at each installed location of the system on confirmation that the product meets the Operations Acceptance Criteria. In the absence of an Operations Manager or the equivalent, it is prepared by the Senior User. In both cases it is signed by the Senior User.
- The User Acceptance Letter is signed by the Senior User(s) of the Project Board when the system has passed the User Acceptance Tests and met User Acceptance Criteria.
- The Business Acceptance Letter is prepared by the Executive of the Project Board at the end of the Project Closure meeting and sent to the IT Executive Committee on confirmation that the other Acceptance Letters have all been signed.

Activity Network
Puts all activities into a logical sequence, showing the dependencies and relationships between the activities. Given an estimate of the duration of each activity, the network shows the total duration of the plan and provides information to assist with the scheduling the work to resources.

Approval to Proceed
Required from the Project Board at Project Initiation and each End-Stage Assessment in order that the project may proceed to the next stage. It represents acceptance of the Stage Plans and a commitment by the Project Board to supply the various resources identified in the Stage Plan.

BAC
See Business Assurance Co-ordinator.

Baseline
The 'freezing' of a Configuration Item, sub-system or the entire system during development so that a known version of it can be either released into production, or to form the firm base of subsequent work. In order to be baselined a Configuration Item must have successfully completed a Quality Review.

Business Acceptance Letter
A letter prepared by the Executive of the Project Board at the end of the Project Closure meeting on confirmation that the other Acceptance Letters have all been signed. It records the completion of the project against its objectives and is sent to the IT Steering Committee who instigated the project.

Business Assurance
This is the process of monitoring actual costs and time usage against the plans, signalling deviations and providing reassurance that the Business Case of the project is still intact.

Business Assurance Co-ordinator
A role within the Project Assurance Team responsible for planning, monitoring and reporting on all business assurance aspects of the project. The role also co-ordinates all Quality Review activities.

Business Case
The justification for undertaking a project, defining the benefits which the project is expected to deliver, the savings it will bring, measured against the costs of implementing the project and running the system.

Chairman
The person in charge of a Quality Review. Supervises the preparation phase, chairs the review. Keeps the momentum going during the review, prevents deviations, non-objective comments and stagnation on any point of disagreement. Ensures all actions are recorded and allocated.

Checkpoint
A technical control conducted on a regular basis, usually weekly. The aim is to gather information on achievements and problems from a stage team, allow the team members to hear what other members are doing, disseminate external information to the team and report back in a written form to the Stage Manager. Normally led by the Team Leader with the Technical and Business Assurance Co-ordinators in attendance.

Checkpoint Report
Provides the information to update plans and create Highlight Reports by the Project Manager for the Project Board. It is produced by Stage Manager or the Business Assurance Co-ordinator with help from the Technical Assurance Co-ordinator. If they have not attended the meeting the report is made out by the Team Leader.

CMM
See Configuration Management Method.

Configuration Librarian
The role which controls the receipt, storage and issue of all products created by the project.

Configuration Management
The process of identifying and describing all the technical components created during the development of the system, controlling the status and change of those items, recording and reporting the status, and maintaining libraries of master copies of the items.

Configuration Management Method
A method to identify all Configuration Items, creating and maintaining libraries to hold the products, plus the procedures to issue and receive the products and report on their status.

Control Points
PRINCE has four control points common to all stages:
- End-Stage Assessment
- Mid-Stage Assessment
- Quality Review
- Checkpoint

See relevant entries in this glossary for more detail.

CRAMM
CCTA Security Risk Analysis and Management Methodology. A complete package which provides a basis to identify and justify all the protective measures necessary to ensure the security of IT systems.

Dependency
A constraint on the sequence and timing of work within a plan.

Detailed Resource Plan
Shows the resources and cost of a Detailed Technical Plan.

Detailed Technical Plan
A stage activity may be so complex or large that it merits a sub plan all to itself to show the breakdown into small work units.

End-Stage Assessment
A management control at the end of each stage, consisting of a formal presentation to the Project Board by the Project Manager of the current project status and the proposed next stage plans. Signed approval by the Project Board is needed before the project can move into the next stage.

ESA
See End-Stage-Assessment.

Exception Plan
Produced in situations where costs and/or timescale tolerances of a stage plan either have been exceeded or can be forecast to be exceeded. It is produced by the Project Manager and presented to the Project Board at a Mid-Stage Assessment.

Executive
A member (usually the Chairman) of the Project Board. The official reporting line to the IT Executive Committee. Specifically responsible for ensuring that the project achieves its expected benefits within its budget and schedule.

Highlight Report
Prepared by the Project Manager for the Project Board at intervals agreed with them when the stage plan was approved. It is based on the Checkpoint Report and covers new achievements, real or potential problems and a forecast of achievements over the next period.

Impact Analysis
The process of assessing the ramifications of a proposed change to the specification, listing what products would be affected by the change and evaluates the size and scope of change to each of the products.

Individual Work Plan
A definition of the tasks, responsibilities and performance measurement of a team member, derived from the Stage Technical Plan and accompanied by a copy of the relevant Product Description.

Informal Review
A Quality Review carried out by two people, the person who created a

product and a reviewer. The three phases of preparation, review and follow-up are still used, but the normal roles will be shared. The presenter would also take the role of scribe, and the reviewer would also act as chairman. These often work best if kept to a review of 30 minutes or less.

IS
Information Systems

IS Steering Committee
The top management group within a department responsible for the overall direction of the IS strategy. It may also be called the IT Strategy Committee.

IT
Information Technology.

IT Executive Committee
The senior management group responsible for overall direction of IT projects and implementation of the IT strategy. It initiates projects, appoints the Project Boards and sets Terms of Reference.

Library
A set of Configuration Items. These may be hardware, software or documentation.

Mid-Stage Assessment
A formal meeting between Project Board and Project Manager held for one or more of the following reasons:
- as an interim assessment of the progress of a long stage
- to authorise limited work to begin on the next stage before the current stage is complete
- to make a decision on an Exception Plan.

MSA
See Mid-Stage Assessment.

Off-Specification Report
Used to document any situation where the system fails to meet its specification in some respect. It is triggered by a Project Issue Report.

Operations Acceptance Letter
Prepared by the Operations Manager at each location where the system is installed after ensuring that the system complies with the Operations Acceptance Criteria.

PAT
See Project Assurance Team.

PBS
See Product Breakdown Structure.

PFD
See Product Flow Diagram.

PIR
See Project Issue Report.

Post Implementation Review
An integral part of the management and control of the project carried out six to twelve months after a system becomes operational. Its purpose is twofold; to check that the system has met its objectives and to check that the system is meeting user needs.

Presenter
At a Quality Review, usually the author of the item under review able to answer questions about the item in order to decide if there are errors or not.

PRINCE
Projects in Controlled Environments. The standard method of project management in government IT departments.

Product
Any final or interim output from a project.

Product Breakdown Structure
Identifies the products which must be produced. It is a hierarchical structure, decomposing the products through a number of levels with three main branches, representing technical, management and quality products.

Product Description
A description of the purpose, composition and quality criteria to be applied to the product. There should be a Product Description for every product.

Product Flow Diagram
Shows the required sequence of the development of the products and the dependencies between them.

Project
A project is regarded as having the following characteristics:
- a defined and unique set of technical products to meet a business need
- a corresponding set of activities to construct those products
- a defined amount of resources
- a finite lifespan
- an organisational structure with defined responsibilities.

Project Assurance Team
Consists of three technical and administrative roles, covering the whole project, and through whom project continuity and integrity are maintained. It comprises Business, Technical and User Assurance Co-ordinators.

Project Board
Consists of three management roles; Executive, Senior User and Senior Technical. One or more people may take each role depending on the interests of the project and the need to supply resources. It is necessary for the appointees to have managerial authority because of the need for them to make commitments.

Project Brief
See Terms of Reference.

Project Closure
The ending of the project requires formal approval and agreement from the Project Board. This may be combined with the End-Stage Assessment of the final stage.

Project Evaluation Review
A documented review of the project's performance, produced for the Project Closure. It ensures that any lessons learned are recorded for the benefit of other projects.

Project Initiation Document
Records the formal, business-like start to a project. It is prepared by the Project Manager and Project Assurance Team and approved by the Project Board. It contains:
- Terms of Reference
- Acceptance Criteria
- Project Organisation and responsibilities
- Project Plans

- First Stage Plans
- Business Case
- Business Risk Assessment
- Product Descriptions
- Project Issue Report

Used as the initial document to raise any and all issues relating to the project apart from an action point from a Quality Review. If it requires action it will lead to either a Request for Change or an Off-Specification Report. If a point is raised during a Quality Review which is outside the scope of that review, it should be submitted on a Project Issue Report.

Project Issue Report
Used to raise issues relating to the project. Its subject can be anything to do with the project, technical or management. It is the means of bringing any question, error or change request to the attention of the project management apart from the items listed on a Quality Review Follow Up Action List or Exception Memo.

Project Resource Plan
Produced for the Project Initiation Document at the start of a project, summarising the resources estimated to be required for the whole project, based on the Project Technical Plan.

Project Support Office
A group of Business and Technical Assurance Co-ordinators supplying those roles to a number of projects.

Project Technical Plan
Produced for the Project Initiation Document at the start of a project, showing the schedule of major activities for the whole project. It is an estimate.

PSO
See Project Support Office.

QA
See Quality Assurance.

Quality Assurance
The establishment of standards and procedures for quality control and the auditing, inspection and review of the procedures themselves, the quality controls carried out and the results obtained.

Quality Control
The examination and checking of products to ensure that they meet standards and their specification.

Quality Criteria
The characteristics of a product which determine whether it meets requirements, thus defining what 'quality' means for that product.

Quality Review
A procedure whereby a product is checked against an agreed set of quality criteria.

Request for Change
A means of proposing a change to the specification of the system. It can only be raised with the approval of the Project Manager after analysis of a Project Issue Report.

Reviewer
The role at a Quality Review which checks that a product meets its quality criteria.

RFC
See Request for Change.

Senior Technical
One of the roles on the Project Board representing the interests of the development resources. In addition the role represents the interests of technical management.

Senior User
A role on the Project Board representing the interests of the affected user community.

Stage
The PRINCE method allows a project to be divided into a number of stages. A stage represents either the amount of work which the Project Manager is confident about planning or how far the Project Board want the project to go before formally checking its progress and viability. The end of a stage is chosen to correspond with the completion of one or more major products.

Stage Manager
The manager of a stage, reporting to the Project Manager; this role may or

may not be used.

Stage Resource Plan
A summary of the resource and cost needs of a stage, based on the Stage Technical Plan.

Stage Team
A composition of the skills needed to develop the products of a particular stage.

Stage Technical Plan
A chart of the technical and quality activities of a stage shown against an appropriate timeframe.

System Acceptance Letter
Prepared by the Project or Stage Manager for signature by the Senior Technical member of the Project Board confirming that the System Acceptance Tests have been successfully passed.

TAC
See Technical Assurance Co-ordinator.

Technical Assurance
The process of monitoring the technical integrity of products.

Technical Assurance Co-ordinator
One of the roles within the Project Assurance Team, responsible for defining technical standards for the various products, then planning, monitoring, advising and reporting on all technical aspects.

Technical Exception
An unplanned situation relating to one or more end products handled initially by creating a Project Issue Report which may lead to a Request For Change or Off-Specification Report.

Terms of Reference
A definition of the objectives for a project, its background, reasons and the constraints on a solution.

Tolerance
The permitted limits above and below a plan's budget and schedule. The Project or Stage Manager has freedom to operate within these limits, but must consult with the Project Board before continuing outside the toler-

ance level. The tolerance is agreed between Project Manager and Project Board on approval of the plan. At a project level the tolerance may have been passed down to the Project Board by the IT Executive Committee.

Transformation
The process of examining the Product Flow Diagram and defining what activities are required to create one product from its predecessors.

UAC
See User Assurance Co-ordinator.

User Acceptance Letter
A letter signed by the Senior User(s) on the Project Board after User Acceptance Tests confirming that the system meets the User Acceptance Criteria.

User Assurance
Protection of the user's interests in a project, ensuring that a full specification of its needs are obtained and that further project work continues to meet that specification.

User Assurance Co-ordinator
A role within the Project Assurance Team responsible for monitoring, advising and reporting on all user aspects of the project; a day-to-day representation of the user on the project.

Index

A

acceptance letters 127

B

baseline 96
business case 67

C

change control 9
checkpoints 20, 87, 205
closure 20, 128
control 19
configuration
   audit 99
   item 96
   management 21, 74,
    91-100
   plan 93
   status accounting 99

D

detailed plan 34, 84
deviation 122

E

estimation 4
end stage assessment 19, 119-
121
exception memo 106
exception plan 18, 124

G

graphical summary 78

H

highlight report 20, 88-90, 207

I

impact analysis 98
individual work plan 34, 84

M

mid-stage assessment 19, 121,
125
monitoring 8

N

network 42

O

off-specification report 114, 215
organisation 22

P

plan 30
   configuration 74, 93
   description 53-55
   detailed 34, 84
   exception 18
   individual work 34